Happy Oops Day, Oops!

# Early Churches of Washington State

# Early Churches of Washington State

Photographs by ARNOLD PEARSON

Text by ESTHER PEARSON

UNIVERSITY OF WASHINGTON PRESS *Seattle and London*

Library of Congress Catalog Card Number 79-1204
ISBN 0-295-95713-1

## Preface

When we set out to do a photographic essay on early churches in Washington State, we had several things in mind. First, we wanted to show, in an interesting and informative way, some representative examples of those still standing today (we were thinking mainly of small-town and rural churches but we later had to make a few important exceptions), and second, we wanted to tell something about the people who built them and the places where they were built. If we could do this we hoped that people would then look at these buildings in a new way—as an important part of our state's history—and the preservation of many would receive new encouragement.

Our photographic efforts were first confined to some churches we had previously been aware of in Snohomish and Skagit counties, not far from our home in Seattle. After we got started, the greater possibilities of what we came to call "the project" became apparent and we decided to include all of western Washington and then, later, also the eastern part. We could now look at these early churches in the context of the history of all of Washington State.

It soon became apparent that we needed a systematic way to identify and locate all these churches. We obtained various denominational publications that listed their churches and the date when each was organized. We checked for early organization dates; for these there was a possibility that the early church building was still standing. We also reviewed church histories, county histories published about the turn of the century, centennial newspapers, and similar publications. In addition we received suggestions from people in towns and areas we visited. All this information provided the leads we needed, but many times when we drove to the locality we were disappointed to find that in place of the hoped-for early church there was a later building or no church at all. This reminded us that there is a continuing attrition of early churches and other old structures, even those of historic importance.

We had to formulate some guidelines on which churches to include. We found and looked at several hundred and there are a great many more we did not see. We could hope to include in a book only a representative fraction of all of these. In general we drew our selection from churches still in use (there are some exceptions) and constructed not later than 1916. We then considered architectural interest, historical importance, and ethnic, denominational, and geographic representation. Because of space limitations we had to make some arbitrary choices, but we believe we do have a group of still-standing churches which is typical of those earlier times. The map on page 180 shows the towns and cities where the churches included here are located.

The photography is a type of architectural photography that has the usual problem of isolating the principal building from any incompatible and distracting elements. This was particularly pertinent here because we had decided the churches should appear in the photographs as much as possible as when they were first built. This meant eliminating or at least minimizing the appearance of today's clutter of power lines and poles, automobiles, contemporary buildings such as service stations, and other evidences of our modern society. We also tried wherever possible to omit or subordinate recent additions or the use of substitute modern materials on the church. Sometimes these problems of modernism affected our selections. At the same time we wanted to emphasize the most interesting features of the church and this might call for a close-up of the steeple, a window, or only a part of the exterior or interior. Both isolation and emphasis were usually accomplished by choosing a particular viewpoint and, if necessary, using a shorter or longer lens on the camera.

Sources for the text material besides those used for initially locating each church were state and local histories, census records, early newspaper articles and photographs, architectural reference books, original writings of missionaries and circuit riders, and denominational publications. Many of these sources are listed in the Bibliography. We also sought specific information directly from each church we planned to include, and this was the major source for the historical data for most churches.

Within our main divisions of Western Washington and Eastern Washington, we have arranged the churches chronologically, referring to the year each church was built (that is, basically completed and put into use). We had difficulty in some cases establishing this date because of conflicting information and, occasionally, confusion with the earlier date the congregation was organized or the later date the church was dedicated. In questionable cases we tried to verify the year built from at least one other source. Where we were not reasonably certain, we have indicated an approximate date.

The church names shown should also be explained. We found that church signs and readerboards were not always current and some gave only the short, familiar name. Even literature from the church sometimes included only the abbreviated name. We finally consulted with a number of denominations for guidance on a consistent approach for their churches.

While working on the project, we attended Sunday services at a few of the churches included in this book to try to get some perception of what it must have been like in those early days. In these small churches, strangers are quickly identified, and we were always warmly and graciously welcomed. One of our most memorable visits was to St. Peter's Episcopal Church in Tacoma for the five o'clock Sunday Vespers. It was already getting dark this November afternoon and a light rain was falling as we entered the dimly lit small church. Inside, we sat down on the wood benches and listened as the lay reader began the service. The world outside, only a few steps away, seemed very remote. As a hymn was played on the old organ and the small congregation sang we thought about other Sunday services held in this church in the settlement of Tacoma one hundred years ago.

Arnold and Esther Pearson
December 1979

vi

## Acknowledgments

We are indebted to the many people—relatives, old friends, new friends, and strangers—who gave us help and encouragement during the years we worked on our "project," the basis for this book.

First we must thank members of the staffs of the Seattle Public Library, Tacoma Public Library, Museum of History and Industry in Seattle, Washington State Historical Museum in Tacoma, Archive House of the Weyerhauser Company, University of Puget Sound Library, Seattle University Library, and Architecture and Suzzallo libraries of the University of Washington who opened their files and guided us to the material we needed. We are especially grateful to Robert Monroe and his colleagues in the Special Collections Division of the Suzzallo Library, where we spent most of our research time.

Puget Sound headquarters of the church denominations represented in this book provided us with information we would have not otherwise been able to obtain. We particularly thank the Reverend Monsignor John P. Doogan, Chancellor of the Archdiocese of Seattle; Dr. Erle Howell, historian of the United Methodist Church; the Reverend Robert L. Moylan of the North Pacific District of the American Lutheran Church; and Mr. William R. Thomas of the Christian Science Committee on Publication.

Without the help of laymen and ministers of the many individual congregations who answered our questionnaires, wrote letters with additional information, sent church histories, or opened the doors of their churches to us we could not have gathered the needed material or completed the photography. In addition, some strangers suggested churches to visit or include. To all these good people, we are deeply thankful.

Finally, we are most grateful to William James, who in the beginning encouraged us and directed us to the University of Washington Press; to Janine Bajus, George Bickford, and Barbara Melton, who read our first draft and offered valuable comments; and especially to Dr. Vernon Carstensen and Professor Daniel Streissguth, whose continual support, suggestions, and encouragement along with that of the staff of the University of Washington Press led to the completion of this book.

# Contents

# Early Churches of Washington State

## Introduction

Many hundreds of churches were built in what is now Washington State during the last half of the nineteenth and the first part of the twentieth centuries—a period from the beginnings of Washington as a territory and continuing into the first decades under statehood. The churches were built to meet not only traditional religious needs but also, as important, the social and community needs of the settlers—at first mostly American citizens and then, later, foreign immigrants.

### 1.

Before these churches were built, missionaries were establishing missions, a few of which survive today. Missionaries came to what was then the Oregon Country beginning in 1834 to teach Indians the white man's religion and way of life. That year at Hudson's Bay Company's Fort Vancouver on the north bank of the Columbia River, Jason Lee, a young Methodist missionary, preached the first sermon in the Pacific Northwest by an ordained minister. In the next few years missionaries of other denominations opened missions among tribes both east and west of the Cascade Mountains. The earliest in Washington State was established in 1836 among the Cayuse tribe near present-day Walla Walla by Dr. Marcus Whitman and his wife Narcissa, who were sent by the combined foreign missions board of the Presbyterian, Congregational, and Dutch Reformed churches. In 1838 the Reverends Elkanah Walker and Cushing Eells, both Congregational ministers, and their wives established their mission, Tshimakain, among the Spokane Indians on the trail between Fort Colville and Fort Walla Walla near present-day Spokane.

The first Catholic priests, Father Francis Norbert Blanchet and Father Modeste Demers, arrived at Fort Vancouver from Montreal in 1838, beginning a long history of work among Northwest Indian tribes. Their earliest mission was St. Francis Xavier, established next to a Hudson's Bay Company farm near present-day Toledo in Lewis County. The first Jesuit missionary to come was Father Pierre Jean DeSmet, who visited Husdon's Bay Company Fort Colville in 1841. St. Paul's at Kettle Falls, built by Father Joseph Joset in 1847, and St. Michael's near Spokane, founded by Father Joseph Cataldo in 1866, were two early Jesuit missions. Oblate missionaries from France arrived at Fort Walla Walla in 1847. They soon established St. Joseph's near Yakima and St. Joseph's at Priest Point near Olympia as well as other stations. In 1858, after the signing of the Indian treaties, Father Eugene Casimir Chirouse was assigned to the Puget Sound mission. This included the Tulalip (his headquarters), Lummi, Swinomish, Port Madison, and Muckleshoot reservations, and the churches built there were the result of his work.

When Congress created Washington Territory in 1853, the new territory included not only the present state of Washington, but also Idaho and parts of Montana and Wyoming. Almost all the population of 3,965, only half of them of voting age, lived in isolated settlements scattered around Puget Sound and along waterways west of the Cascades. Most of them made their living harvesting fish and oysters or producing timber products for shipment to San Francisco, the center of California gold rush activity.

Territorial status brought a few ministers to the Pacific Northwest. Church people were interested in promoting home missions to maintain a cultural tie with the East, to combat the perceived lawlessness and immorality of the West, and to help provide a religious and secular education for the white settlers. The Methodists were the first to send ministers to the area, just as they had been first to send missionaries to the Oregon Country.

The first church for white settlers was built at Steilacoom in 1853. An interesting story about that first church is told by Dr. Erle Howell in *Methodism in the Northwest:*

> Captain Lafayette Balch, founder of Steilacoom, as a rival of Olympia, was ambitious to gain prestige for his town. When, in 1853, he learned that Rev. John F. DeVore had been assigned to Olympia and that, on his way to his charge from the East, the minister would pause briefly at Alki Point, Seattle, the Captain gathered a party of his friends, paddled a canoe, a trip requiring two or three days, to the Point to meet the new minister. They told him that Olympia already had a minister, presiding elder Benjamin Close, and that smallpox was epidemic there. They said Steilacoom offered greater opportunities. De-Vore, a man of action as well as wisdom, passed a subscription paper among his new friends, asking them to pledge what they would give toward a new church at Steilacoom. Then the passengers and crew of the ship were solicited. Being satisfied with the response, the clergyman resolved to accompany them. He organized a congregation the first day and built that year the first church north of the Columbia River.

The two-story building was used for many years as both a church and a school. Although it no longer stands, a plaque erected by the Washington State Historical Society marks the site. The oldest standing Catholic church in the state is also at Steilacoom. Originally built in 1856 on the grounds of Fort Steilacoom as a chapel for the soldiers, it was moved several years later to the town, where it was dedicated in 1864.

The Reverend David Blaine of New York and his wife Catherine were also sent to serve at Puget Sound in 1853. They expected to serve at Steilacoom, but since that charge was already filled they went to Seattle instead. At first they were unable to build a church because there were too few people and they had little money to help pay for it. Rivalry between citizens also delayed locating the church.

Catherine wrote to her family, "Each is afraid that the other will have some preference shown him or will derive more than his share of the benefit from the locality of the church. . . ." Once given the land, the minister himself labored: "In order to get a place to put our house [of worship] he had to clear off land more thickly wooded than any of which you ever dreamed. . . ." Two years later, in May 1855, she wrote:

> We had our dedication last Sunday. All went off pleasantly, notwithstanding the day was very rainy and unfavorable. . . . After the sermon Mr. Blaine offered the dedicatory prayer and then proceeded to raise money to pay off the debt on the house. . . . [He] designs to go on and try to raise enough to paint it and finish the inside. He will probably finish the inside by ceiling with planed boards, as plaster is very liable to crack and fall off on account of the lath swelling and shrinking by reason of the damp weather. . . . It is 24×36 feet in width and 14 foot posts. . . . At the other end of the room is the pulpit, which is small and neat. On each side of the pulpit are three seats. There is but one aisle, a center one three feet wide. The house would comfortably seat 150 persons. . . . On the top in front is a low square steeple, designed for a bell as soon as the people can afford to buy one. When the house is painted it will be quite an ornament to the town.

Several other Methodist churches were organized at this time in the territory. The small church built in 1858 at Claquato (near Chehalis), once a thriving village on the Military Road between Fort Steilacoom and Fort Vancouver, was dedicated by the Methodists. It is the oldest Protestant church now standing in Washington State.

While a few churches and missions were built during the first years of the territory (the 1860 census listed twelve), the early settlers spent most of their energy and effort establishing themselves in their new surroundings. They cleared and drained land, built houses and barns, planted and harvested their gardens, and worked at a variety of jobs to earn a cash income. They had little time or opportunity to enjoy social activities or to participate in organized religion.

During the early 1860s there was actually a decline in church growth in the Pacific Northwest. This was due in part to the discovery of gold in British Columbia as well as east of the Cascade Mountains, which not only drew a transient mining population of thousands to the area but also attracted local people who sought to get rich quickly. Mining towns were usually temporary; miners were ready to move on as new strikes were discovered elsewhere. There was little interest or time for religious activity in this environment.

The Civil War also had a negative effect on church growth. Even though Washington Territory was far removed from the conflict, the war influenced the economic, political, and social life of the new territory, and church growth and missionary work diminished. Church societies in eastern states were no longer interested in the West, but were thinking of the needs of people directly affected by the war. Young men who ordinarily would have trained for the ministry were needed to fight. In addition, some of the ministers who had earlier come west returned to serve as chaplains.

When the war ended and the country was again at peace, people once more looked to the West. In addition, a religious revival in the East stimulated missionary, Bible, and tract societies to again send men and money. There were few priests and trained ministers available, however, and some who came were not ordained. All were assigned large areas to serve. The Reverend Peter Hyland, an Episcopalian, was given the Puget Sound area as his charge in 1865; at times he was the only clergyman of his denomination in Washington Territory. The Methodists had more ministers at that time, two for the Walla Walla district and six for western Washington. These men and others were assigned to work in areas that in some cases had no known church members. The difficulties of travel were also great. The few early roads were little more than deeply rutted trails, and in western Washington often through dense forests. Bridges over rivers and streams were almost nonexistent. Most travelers favored water travel, using canoes, other small craft, and steamboats to carry them to settlements.

All through this early period, Catholic missionaries had continued to work with the many Indian tribes on their reservations, living in the most primitive of conditions. In 1864 Father F. X. Prefontaine came to the territory, one of the first priests sent to serve the white settlers. His district included all the islands of the Sound, the northeastern Olympic Peninsula, Port Gamble, Seattle, and all the mainland east of the Sound to British Columbia.

Missionaries, visiting priests, and ministers first held services in private homes, schools, rooms over stores and even over saloons, various halls, or churches already established by other congregations. In a few communities, the people who met regularly began church construction before they were assigned a regular minister. When the Reverend Peter Hyland first started serving the area that included Port Townsend, he found a church building, later consecrated as St. Paul's Episcopal Church, almost completed. At Port Gamble, the mill company town, the church built in 1870 was used as a town meeting hall until its dedication as a Congregational church in 1879.

There were a few other cases like these, but usually a minister was sent where no church or parsonage awaited him. He came to the area, located a few interested people, and took an active role in generating enthusiasm for building a church.

The minister often took the lead in soliciting donations for the church building. Leading citizens or pillars of the church were asked to give a site for the church, gifts of money, or building materials. Occasionally challenges were made that enlivened fund-raising activities. When Captain Clanrick Crosby, a mill owner from Tumwater, was asked by the minister to donate to the Methodist church in Olympia, Crosby told him he would give all the lumber the minister could carry to Olympia in one day. The minister arrived at the mill, loaded enough lumber on a raft to build the church, and, with a favorable tide, brought it to the building site the same day.

It was not always easy to get local financing in a building campaign. In many rural areas there was no citizen of wealth to make a generous contribution. Church extension societies in the East recognized the financial plight of the early congregations and provided funds. Loans of a few hundred dollars, to be repaid at a later date, often made the difference as to whether or not a church could be built.

Sometimes the priest or minister was designer as well as builder of the church. Father Prefontaine moved from Port Townsend to Seattle in 1867. By 1869 he had completed a new church for which he was architect, carpenter, painter, and carver of stucco work. In 1872 he built the first Catholic church in LaConner. The Reverend James McNemee, a Methodist preacher known as "Brother Mack," built six churches, finished and dedicated two, repaired six others, and built a parsonage during his many years of preaching in remote areas of Washington. L. F. Stephen, a Disciples of Christ preacher, was a contractor before his conversion. As an evangelist he organized churches, and served congregations as architect and builder.

Usually, building the church was a cooperative effort on the part of the community, which contributed money, materials, and/or labor. Church people and nonbelievers, men, women, and children joined together to complete the project. When Presbyterians at Port Townsend built the first stone church north of the Columbia, the whole community helped haul the stones, which were gathered from nearby areas.

Completion of the church in a settlement lifted the spirits of the people. It was not only a place for worship, but also a place for fellowship; it became a link between their primitive environment of the present and the more civilized life most of them left behind. Now there was a proper setting for religious service, and a place for participation in the joyous church rituals of baptism, confirmation, and marriage, as well as the somber services for the dead—in the frontier community, death came early to many. It provided a center for community celebrations of holidays, especially at Christmas, when for some there was a large decorated tree and garlands of cedar greens ornamented with red paper bells, a children's program, the singing of carols, and the distribution of gifts and candy and fruit treats in small mesh bags. For others, there was the special midnight service in the tradition of the church.

Some churches were fortunate enough to have an organ, usually shipped around the Horn in a sailing vessel as was the pump organ for St. Peter's Episcopal Church in Tacoma in 1874. In Naches, one family brought its Estey organ to church in a wagon for special occasions and musical entertainment. The sound of the church organ was sometimes the only instrumental music the settlers heard other than the small instruments they might have brought with them.

Sunday in the more stable settlements was the day to put aside the rough utilitarian clothes worn during the week and to "dress up." For some it meant a wagon ride to the nearby town, to meet together in worship service, and then to have a basket social or picnic dinner in the church or church yard afterwards. It was a time especially important for the women of the frontier. Because government land grants were large and land was cheap, many settlers had large acreages and distances between neighbors could be very great, particularly in the dry lands of eastern Washington. West of the Cascades distances might not be so great, but travel was difficult and farms and villages there were also quite isolated.

There were few public meeting places for the respectable woman in the frontier community. The church provided a center for social events and a chance for women to work and to be together. They held teas, church suppers, musicals, and bazaars and fairs where needlework, preserves, and baked specialties could be put on display and sold. All these activities gave women a chance to meet together, to visit, to exchange ideas and gossip, and to encourage each other as well as benefit the church. Through such efforts women raised money to buy gifts for the church such as the bell, organ, and pews, or even to help pay the minister's salary or the church debt, or to build and furnish a parsonage.

The church in the community also gave interested men a chance to demonstrate and develop leadership roles as they organized a congregation, conducted finance campaigns, helped with building construction, or served as lay leaders in church services or on church governing boards.

In addition the church benefited the community as a whole in both practical and less tangible ways. Often the building was used for a school before schoolhouses were built. The minister, and some-

times his wife, was considered well qualified to teach the children in pioneer settlements, and the tuition paid augmented the small income received from mission societies and the congregation. Many denominations also built academies to provide higher education for young people, some of which were the foundation of colleges and universities that exist today.

The church building was a symbol of permanence and stability in frontier settlements. It showed that there were settlers who respected morality and law, who wanted to keep traditions and teachings of the past, to educate their children, and to improve their present environment. Often this was important in attracting newcomers with families, especially in those times and areas where there was a large transient population, typically single men working in logging, fishing, and mining.

3.

By the late 1870s Washington Territory had grown slowly but steadily and had a substantial number of small settlements. West of the Cascades there were lumber-mill and mining towns, a few farm settlements, and oystering and fishing villages. East of the mountains there were rural settlements in the wheat and grazing lands near the largest town in the territory, Walla Walla, which had a population of 3,588. In its first thirty years the territory had gained about 74,000 residents, the vast majority native-born Americans.

In the next thirty years a great flood of foreign-born immigrants along with greatly increased numbers of Americans would increase the population of Washington to fifteen times that number. The first foreign-born immigrants to come in large numbers were northern Europeans beginning in the 1880s, followed by southern and eastern Europeans after 1890. This great influx of newcomers to Washington was triggered by the intensive recruiting by the railroads of foreign-born immigrants both in this country and in Europe and the completion of the northern transcontinental railroads.

Like many earlier immigrants to Washington, the foreign born had religious and social needs best satisfied through the church. In addition they had the problems of adjusting to a strange new country with a language different from their own. In the old state churches they left behind, the rites of baptism frequently signified citizenship in the state. The church, and its other rites of confirmation, marriage, and death, had been a dominant part of their daily lives for generations. In America, where there was no state church, the immigrants had to provide for their own religious needs.

In some cases a minister came with the settlers and church services were part of the community from the start. A group of German-Russians who came from Nebraska in 1883 by wagon train over the Oregon Trail to Ritzville, where they settled, were led by their minister, and they always stopped their travel to observe the sabbath. Scandinavian settlers in Washington were first served by a Norwegian Lutheran pastor, the Reverend Christian Jorgenson, who joined the early immigrants who had begun clearing, draining, and diking the delta lands of the Skagit, Stillaguamish, and Snohomish rivers. At Stanwood he built his own home and organized a congregation. The Snohomish newspaper *Northern Star* reported in 1879:

> The new church building at Stanwood by the Norwegians of the Stillaguamish is the first Norwegian Lutheran church ever built on this coast, north of San Francisco. The main part of the church is 24 by 36 feet, with 14 feet posts. . . . It will be finished out side and in with rustic. No joists overhead, ceiling arched etc. . . . The outside will be finished this month, the finishing of the inside will be deferred until next fall.

The building of this and other Lutheran churches drew many new Scandinavian immigrants to nearby settlements.

Churches of foreign immigrants became centers in the community, both providing for religious and social needs and preserving native languages and rituals. Hearing familiar words and songs was important to those who had come so many miles to the Pacific Northwest and knew they would never return to their native soil. In the church, children could be taught the traditions of the homeland; some churches established parochial schools to maintain their ethnic unity. At the same time some of these churches offered second services in English and gave instruction to adults to help them learn the new language.

American churches also extended their missionary work to include foreign immigrants. Almost all American Protestant denominations—Adventist, Baptist, Congregational, Disciples of Christ, Methodist, Presbyterian, and Episcopal—conducted services in one or more foreign languages, including Swedish, Norwegian, Danish, Welsh, German, and Chinese.

The westward movement of great numbers of American pioneers, many of whom had little formal education or church connection, and large numbers of foreign immigrants with close ties to their state churches brought about in the East a new revival of religious fervor and missionary zeal. Once again home mission societies of all Protestant denominations were eager to send help to the Pacific Northwest to provide for religious and educational needs. They sent ministers and teachers and paid part of their salaries. They provided hymnals and publications for Sunday schools as well as gifts of money and loans to build churches. For example, the Methodists established a "Frontier Fund" with an appeal for $250 donations which would be given along with $1,200 loans to build rural churches. They also provided the plans for church buildings they felt were suitable for the congregation.

Even though a greater number of ministers came to Washington there still were not enough to serve the entire territory. Thus the practice of "circuit riders," which had been used primarily by the Methodists throughout the United States for almost seventy years, increased in the 1880s. A circuit rider was a minister assigned to a specific area where he organized and visited different congregations on a regular schedule. He might conduct Sunday services at five or six churches, preaching in each once or twice a month, morning, afternoon, or evening. The circuit system was used by most denominations and in effect continues today in some places where several small congregations share a minister.

There were also the itinerant preachers or missionaries who traveled even greater distances, seeking out recent settlers and organizing Sunday schools and congregations. The Reverend George Kennedy, who began preaching in eastern Washington in the 1870s and traveled an estimated eighty thousand miles in forty years of service, wrote:

> The itinerant preacher: The pathfinder, trailmaker, cabin home hunter, stream swimmer, preacher to the many or the few along the trails, sleeping on the pile of brush or the straw tick, sitting at the rude table to the coarse wheat cake and venison stew.

The Reverend George Atkinson made frequent trips from Portland to Spokane to establish Congregational churches and Sunday schools in eastern Washington. In 1882, with six local people, he organized a church in the new town of Ritzville. Preachers of all denominations traveled, usually on horseback, the wheat and grazing lands of southeastern Washington and the dry mountains and canyons near Yakima, Ellensburg, Chelan, and Colville, or they journeyed by stagecoach along roads deep with dust in the intense heat of day and the chill of night. Winter snow and cold brought additional hardship. One preacher went to a meeting eight miles from Dayton in subzero weather. After staying overnight with a settler, he and his host saddled horses and rode in the bitter cold to a schoolhouse about two miles away. Though almost frozen, they were able to start a fire and thaw out; about a dozen people came to the meeting.

Some who were assigned stations on the Olympic Peninsula walked the shoreline, scrambling up steep banks covered with brush and trees to escape the high tide and surf. Others, sometimes wearing hipboots, struggled across the tide lands and marshes of the flat river deltas still being diked and drained, such as the Baptist preacher in the early 1880s who walked the nine miles from his church in Mount Vernon to his other church in LaConner. The Reverend John Tennant's assignment in 1885 was the San Juan Islands. He made his rounds from Eastsound on Orcas Island to Lopez and San Juan islands by rowboat, a ten- to fifteen-mile trip over waters that were cold and usually rough and treacherous. To meet settlers he walked several miles inland over island trails. For this he received a one-year salary of one hundred dollars from missionary funds and thirty-six dollars from offerings of the settlers. In spite of all the hardships and the low pay he asked to be returned to this circuit for another year.

During the thirty years following the completion of the first northern transcontinental railroad, most of the thousands of immigrants who came to Washington settled near others of the same ethnic or religious heritage, whether they came as individuals, small groups, or colonies. Eastern Washington attracted German-Russians and Germans—Catholics and Lutherans, Mennonites, and other Protestant groups. Ethnic concentrations included Swedes and Finns along the Columbia River and in Lewis County; Norwegians and Swedes in

9

Kitsap, Skagit, and Snohomish counties; the Dutch on Whidbey Island, around Lynden in Whatcom County, and near Yakima; English and Canadians near the border and in the Okanogan Valley; and Swiss-Germans at Frances in Pacific County and near Napavine in Lewis County. Most of the Jews who came to the Northwest settled in urban areas, although a small number joined the several communal agricultural colonies in the Puget Sound area. American Blacks settled principally in Seattle, Tacoma, and Spokane, and in the mining communities of Roslyn and Franklin.

After 1890 the immigration to Washington included not only many Americans, Canadians, and northern Europeans, but also greatly increasing numbers of Asians, Jews, Italians, Austrians, Slavs, Poles, and Greeks. The Asians and southern and eastern Europeans did not face some of the physical hardships the pioneer settlers suffered during territorial days. But because many of them had little education and had difficulty with the language, laws, and customs of this country, their first years in their new homeland were also hard. In the general community their differences in dress, speech, and manners made it difficult for the newcomers.

Like other national groups who came earlier, the new immigrants sought others who had a common background and either formed communities or established neighborhoods in larger towns and cities where they spoke their native language in the home, stores, fraternal organizations, and their nearby church. In Seattle many early Italian immigrants settled near Rainier Avenue and surrounding areas. Devout Catholics, they attended St. Boniface, a National German church that had served German Catholics beginning in 1890. The Germans gradually moved away, and after 1909 Jesuits served the church. After the Italians petitioned Rome to send an Italian priest, Father Louis Caramello of Turin came in 1913. Soon Our Lady

of Mount Virgin was built as church and school to provide religious services and a free education for Italian immigrant children as well as to preserve the language and some of the traditions of the homeland.

The first Sephardic (Spanish-Portugese) Jewish immigrants came to Seattle from the eastern Mediterranean region in 1903. Others joined them, settling in the neighborhood of the Orthodox Bikur Cholim Synagogue. When that congregation moved to larger quarters the Sephardim bought the building. By 1916 there were approximately fifteen hundred Sephardim in Seattle, becoming the third largest community of Sephardic Jews in the United States. Their first synagogue no longer stands.

Tacoma, the terminus of the Northern Pacific Railroad, drew immigrants of many nations, including Lithuanians, Slovaks, and Italian-speaking Yugoslav fishermen and miners. A large number of Polish families settled in South Tacoma and along Portland Avenue near the mills, smelters, and railroads where they worked and in the nearby Puyallup Valley. Many Poles also settled at Pe Ell in Lewis County. At the request of Catholics there in 1892, a Polish-speaking priest came to serve them, and in 1893 St. Joseph's Church was dedicated. In 1916 Holy Cross Polish National Catholic Church was also organized and built there.

The decade after the turn of the century brought not only an increase in population, but also a great increase in church membership and church construction for all denominations in the growing cities and rural communities. In most communities "almost everyone goes to church," and many of the socially prominent and respectable businessmen and their families attended regularly. The large number of foreign immigrants who settled in Washington State, especially those from southern and eastern Europe, were to a considerable degree responsible for this increased church activity. By

1910, twenty-one different languages were spoken in Washington churches, and the number of foreign language churches was exceeded only in Minnesota, Wisconsin, and the Dakotas. That year the Indian Shaker Church, an organization combining rituals of the Catholic, Protestant, and Indian religions and founded in 1881 by John Slocum, a Squaxin Indian, was formally incorporated in the state of Washington. None of their earliest churches remain standing today.

Even though many communities of Washington changed rapidly from frontier settlements to cities and towns with brick business sections, fine homes and large churches, street railway systems and electricity, there were still vast areas of the state that were sparsely settled and remote from urban centers, especially in eastern Washington. Like the earliest ministers and circuit riders, the missionary preachers traveled long distances to meet with settlers and organize Sunday schools in rural settlements. The Reverend W. O. Forbes reported that in seven and one-half years of missionary work in the Central Washington and Walla Walla presbyteries, an area almost as large as Pennsylvania, he organized one hundred Sunday schools. Out of these grew twenty-eight Presbyterian church organizations plus eight churches of other denominations. The following description of his travels in the early 1900s reflects the contrasting blend of the worldly pleasures and modern travel of the day with the traditional missionary work on horseback:

> The work abounds in interesting experiences. One year ago I went in on the first train that carried passengers on the Milwaukee railway from Lind to Othello, a divisional point on that road in Adams County. It was a company going there to a Saturday night dance, the first dance in the new town. The next day I preached the first sermon and organized the first Sunday School in a tent on the block and at the same hour with their first baseball game. The baseball game was followed by "bronco busting" and horse racing, attended with music by a brass band. I preached again in the evening, with many present who had part in the morning festivities. That is the way the first Easter Sunday in Othello was spent. Today we have a good church organization, with a nice church all paid for, and a "sky pilot" in charge of the work. . . .
>
> I took a scouting tour of 100 miles on horseback in Klickitat County, distributing literature to the scattered families. I found one family of five children, the oldest a girl not more than 12 years old, that wanted a Sunday School organized in their neighborhood. Nearby were a number of homesteaders on timbered land, all of whom were struggling for a living. The Sabbath School was organized. I went back a year later and found that they had not missed a Sunday in the whole year, though the snow was sometimes from four to five feet deep. At this meeting they were worshiping in a grove out in the open. A year later, on another visit, I found the people holding services in a private house. . . . The next year when I went back they had a little chapel they had built with their own hands, having but $150 in money. . . .

In 1911, one hundred years after overland fur traders had built Fort Okanogan, their first trading post north of the Columbia, Washington was the thirteenth most populous state in the Union. A 1916 survey showed that it ranked twenty-seventh in number of church members, compared to forty-sixth in 1890, with 2,364 church buildings, an increase of over 600 in ten years. The next decade would show a slower rate of immigration into the state, a slowdown in church construction, and a lower percentage of the population claiming church membership. Several factors of national and international significance were responsible for this.

An estimated thirty-two million immigrants came to America in the hundred years ending in 1914, the year over one million people crossed the Atlantic. The outbreak of World War I, however, slowed immigration dramatically; fewer than two hundred thousand Europeans came to America in 1915 and at the same time many aliens returned to their homelands.

The advent of large numbers of automobiles also

11

had a profound effect. When Henry Ford brought assembly-line techniques to automobile manufacture, ownership of a car came within the reach of almost everyone. As more people bought cars, more and better highways were built, making it possible to move about easily for business and pleasure. The church became less important in the social life of the community. Church members could also choose to drive to larger communities to attend services. Many congregations in formerly isolated areas joined together, causing many small churches to close. World War I also adversely affected church growth. The emphasis was on the war effort, not on church building. Many foreign language churches lost members to English language denominations or changed their own services to show their patriotism.

With all that has been said here about the religious activity and church growth in Washington in the late 1800s and early 1900s, it should not be inferred that the church was a dominant influence in the growth and development of the state. A majority of the pioneers and settlers had no religious affiliations. But even for those the church provided a stabilizing influence and helped to set a moral tone in the new and often rough civilization that was struggling to survive and to grow. Along with the family and the school, the church provided the basic strength and sense of integrity that were needed to establish a permanent community. And for those with church ties, especially the foreign immigrants, the church, in addition to serving their religious needs, was an anchor, something to hold on to, and sometimes their only tie with their past in this strange new land. Today, the pioneers and immigrants who are still alive, their descendants, and modern-day immigrants can look with respect and pride on those early church structures, built, often with great effort and sacrifice, during the early years of Washington.

Significant numbers of those early churches still stand and include examples by different denominations from different time periods and geographic areas. A general survey can thus be made of the basic construction and certain details of these church buildings and some of the factors that influenced their design.

Certainly one of the most obvious influences in the basic construction and decoration was the availability and cost of materials, particularly in the early years of the period when most congregations had little money and transportation of materials was difficult. Wood, of course, was the cheapest, most readily available, and most easily worked material; sawmills were often in or near the community in which the church was to be built, and wood was the standard material for homes and, until later years, for some fairly large buildings. Moreover, besides the skilled carpenters employed, some of the volunteer labor that was usually necessary had experience in working with wood, having built their own houses and barns. A few early churches were built of brick or stone, principally in eastern Washington or in the larger communities of the western part. But wood was used in the vast majority of churches built during the period covered by this book and greatly influenced and sometimes limited the general plan, structure, and ornamental design possible. The principal kinds of wood available were the giant Douglas firs and cedars in the western part of the state and pine east of the mountains and in Idaho.

Another important factor was the dedication and financial resources of the members, and, sometimes more important, the support received from the general community. In thinly settled rural areas where the members were still struggling to survive, a church built with only the members' efforts, plus a small amount of help from the denominational headquarters, was likely to be a modest, basic shelter with only those functional design features and ornamentation necessary to identify it as a church. In the more populous areas and especially in towns of relative affluence, such as mill towns, where community leaders gave their support, the design was generally much more refined and included more ornamentation. The church at Port Gamble is an outstanding early example.

Denominational differences, especially in the small rural churches, were minor except in their interior decoration and furnishings. There was a certain consistency in the centering of the steeple at the front of Catholic churches, the austerity of many of the Methodist churches, the Anglican heritage of the Episcopal churches. But if a layman were to stop in front of one of these early churches, it would be difficult in most cases for him to identify with certainty the denomination merely from the exterior design.

The ethnic background of the congregation that built a church is also usually not apparent in the general exterior design. Some churches, however, have design features that do show a particular European influence. The bell tower of the Pioneer Church in Odessa easily suggests the German-Russian background of the builders. The massive twin towers of the Catholic church in Uniontown reflect the Germanic origin of the settlers in the area. The belfry and the general style of the Catholic church in the Rainier Valley of Seattle reflect the Italian heritage of the first priest and congregation. And, of course, the onion dome on the Orthodox church in Wilkeson shows the influence of the Slavic immigrants there.

There was only limited development and refinement of small rural church styles from the 1850s to 1910. The very first Protestant church built in Washington was at Steilacoom in 1853 (no longer standing) and was patterned after the New England meeting house of the early 1800s. This type of building had two stories, a gently sloping roof, a square bell tower centered at the front of the roof, and plain glass rectangular windows. A few years later the Catholic church in Steilacoom and the Methodist churches in Seattle and Claquato, although much smaller, retained some of the character of the New England style. In the following years most rural church design included some forms and details derived from the Gothic, including the feeling of height, the pointed arch, and pinnacles. But if there was any significant development of small church architecture, it was not consistent and not particularly related to time. A church built in a small community of modest resources in 1905 could be very much like a church built in a similar community forty years earlier. Thus, the development of church design was affected mostly by individual circumstances and the capabilities of the individual designers and builders.

In the early years of the period, few professional architects were employed to design a specific church for a selected site as is done as a matter of course today. For one thing there were few local architects available. The 1884 Polk business directory listed only nine architectural firms for all of Washington Territory. For another it was simpler and less expensive for the small and financially limited congregations to use other methods. Sometimes the pastor, priest, or church leaders worked out the general plan, style, and type and degree of ornamentation; experienced carpenters and builders, knowledgeable in house and small-building construction, could determine the type of structure required, sizes of structural members, and door and window details. Many times the carpenters were ingenious and skillful in creating ornamental details in the steeple, windows, and interior, working with wood, often their only available material. In some cases standard plans were obtained from church extension societies in the East. The Methodist Application for Aid (loan or grant) required a description of the proposed church design. Typical entries found in some original applications include "building wood, see plan 28" and "wood frame, Style No. 40, B. T. Price Architect." These standard plans were slightly modified to suit local needs and tastes. Thus the churches at Bayview, Bay Center (no longer standing), and Oysterville, although different in details, appear to be built from the same basic plan. The Eagle Harbor (Bainbridge Island) church used a standard design of a New England Congregational church.

The use of trained architects became more prevalent beginning in the late 1880s, especially in the more populous cities like Seattle, Tacoma, and Spokane where most of the larger and more costly churches were built. The structural problems alone of these more complex and sophisticated designs, often of brick or stone, required trained professionals. But even into the early 1900s the small rural church in Washington State continued to be designed by nonprofessionals or adapted from standard plans. While some of these small churches were not well proportioned, had inconsistent detailing styles, and used garish ornamentation, they probably did reflect more directly and honestly the tastes, values, and cultural background of the church members than if the church had been professionally designed by an outsider.

In the actual design, most of the early churches and also those built later in rural areas were small in size, rectangular in plan, with a fairly steeply pitched gable roof, and with a steeple or belfry centered at the front end. The entrance was also usually centered at the front and faced the street or road. This orientation was probably dictated, more than anything else, by the shape of the building site, often a small narrow lot, that was available

at a reasonable cost or was donated. As a result the typical early church might face in any compass direction. Some churches were built on corner or large lots, which allowed more variations in design, such as L-shaped plans and corner steeples and entrances, as well as permitting more flexibility in orienting the church on the lot. Churches in small, early towns were usually located at least a block away from the main business street to maintain some distance from the saloons there.

Most of the early frame churches had wood post foundations, or large timbers were laid directly on the ground, although many of these were changed in later years to stone or concrete, sometimes when a basement was added or the church was moved to a new site. For the frame churches, bevel or drop siding with corner boards was almost universal. The roof was covered with cedar shingles, which were hand made until shingle machines came into use in 1886. Two or three standard size windows were provided on each side of the smaller churches, up to four or five in the larger churches. A variety of window shapes was used in different churches: rectangular, Gothic pointed arch, and Roman semicircular arch, usually divided into smaller lights. In a few churches, the Gothic-style windows were angular instead of arched at the top, probably to simplify construction. The old Methodist church at Stanwood has this type of window. The windows of these different shapes were generally double hung and glazed with clear glass, although there was some use of stained or frosted glass. Large stained-glass windows were uncommon except in the larger churches later in the period. Occasionally, however, moderate-size decorative round windows divided in a rose or quatrefoil pattern were used.

The greatest variety in the exterior design of the early churches is found in the steeple and belfry. One of the most prevalent design approaches was to place the steeple at the front of the church on an attached four-sided enclosed structure that extended to ground level. Sometimes only part of this structure projected from the church front. The projecting enclosure also provided space for a small vestibule outside the main plan of the church. Another popular style was to center the steeple or a cupola belfry on the roof near its front edge. Within these two general approaches was a wide variety of steeple styles, from tall and thin to short and squat. Cupola belfries were often almost identical in external appearance to barn cupolas. Louvers were usually used to cover the Gothic, Roman, or rectangular openings in the belfry. If there was a spire it was most often surmounted by a cross or decorative finial of wood or metal.

Beginning in the 1880s fancy-cut shingles were used on the steeple, front, and sides of many churches. The shingle ends were cut to half circle, arc, diamond, square, or other shapes and laid in rows; sometimes there were alternate rows of different-shaped ends. Shingles of this type were also widely used on Victorian houses of the era and represented an ingenious and inexpensive way to use wood in a decorative manner. Other examples of carpenter art with wood included ornamental posts made on a turning lathe and used in belfry openings, trefoil and quatrefoil cutouts, elaborate brackets, pinnacles on the steeple base and roof corners, and pediments over windows.

Most of the early frame churches still standing today are painted white and this was the color generally used on the early New England style churches. As church design moved toward freer and more decorative styles, however, color was widely used not only for the color itself, but to emphasize structural details, general trim, and the space divisions created by panels of fancy-cut shingles and other wood patterns. Occasionally, horizontal bands of different colors were applied

to the upper part of the church and steeple to create entirely new patterns. Color, like fancy shingles and cutouts, was a simple and inexpensive way to decorate and to give some individuality to a church.

St. Mary's Catholic Church in Coupeville (originally Congregational) is a good example that can be seen today since it was recently repainted in its original 1889 colors. These include light yellow siding, brown trim, and bands of white, yellow, and brown on the shingles at the gable ends, and white on the belfry shingles and posts.

Although the church interiors varied considerably, most had a basic rectangular plan with the altar or chancel at the end opposite the entry and with rows of pews separated by a center aisle. Most ceilings were closed in but there was some use of exposed roof truss beams finished in a dark stain. The beams ranged in design from the simple scissors truss in the log St. Andrew's Episcopal Church in Chelan to the Gothic arch style in St. Paul's Episcopal Church in Port Townsend. The beam designs were often embellished with cutouts or by carving, as in the Methodist church in Montesano, or by more elaborate carved and turned parts. The treatment of walls and ceilings included painted tongue and groove boards, or cloth or paper pasted to the boards and then painted. Later, plastered walls and ceilings were used extensively. A wainscoting of dark stained vertical boards along the sides and back was fairly common.

The interior furnishings reflected more than any other design characteristic the church denomination: the Roman Catholic elaborate statuary and altar, the Episcopalian symbols and altar, the Lutheran altar and altar rail, and the general austerity of the Methodist, Baptist, and fundamentalist denominations.

In looking at the pictures which follow, or better yet, inspecting the churches in person, one should remember that all of them have been modified in one way or another since they were first built. Necessary functional changes have been made, such as the replacement of wood-burning stoves with modern heating plants, electric lights in place of the original candles or kerosene lamps, and modernized wiring and plumbing. Structural modifications have also been necessary in some cases, including concrete foundations and the addition of iron tie rods in the exposed beam ceilings to prevent spreading of the walls. In addition many of the churches have been enlarged, ceilings have been lowered, stained glass memorial windows installed, Sunday school rooms, social halls, and kitchens added, and vestibules provided at the front entrance. In many cases these modifications have been accomplished and materials selected with sensitivity and in keeping with the character of the original design wherever this was at all practical. In other cases not much thought has been given to preserving the integrity of the original design, and substitute modern materials have been used unnecessarily. Asphalt shingles in place of cedar shingles or shakes, corrugated plastic roofs over new entries, modern wall board and accoustical tiles in ceilings are some obvious examples. This is particularly unfortunate because traditional materials and design would generally have performed as well and at little or no greater cost. It has been gratifying, however, to see that an increasing number of congregations are becoming aware of the historical significance of their heritage and are taking steps to preserve and enhance it, not only for themselves but also for future generations. It is hoped that this trend continues because these early church structures, though sometimes simple and unrefined, represent an important part of the pioneer history of the state of Washington.

# WESTERN WASHINGTON CHURCHES

*Immaculate Conception*
*Catholic Church*    1856
STEILACOOM, PIERCE COUNTY

This small frame building is the oldest standing church in the state of Washington. It originally stood near the parade grounds of Fort Steilacoom, the first United States Army post north of the Columbia, established in 1849 after a skirmish between white settlers and Indians. Probably it was built under the supervision of Lieutenant A. V. Kautz, constructing quartermaster in charge of erecting fort buildings from 1855 to 1858. The 23-by-55-foot building includes a parish hall at the rear, a porch, and an attached corner bell tower. The exterior fir clapboard siding is painted white as are the interior walls and ceiling, which are board and batten construction.

The building was erected as a chapel for soldiers and nearby residents and was served by Catholic priests. When the fort was about to be abandoned, Brigadier General William S. Harney gave the building to Sergeant Francis Dean, who, with the help of others, hauled it on skids, a section at a time, to the town of Steilacoom, at that time the most active port on Puget Sound. The church, first called St. Michael the Archangel, was dedicated the Immaculate Conception Church by Bishop A. M. A. Blanchet in 1864. For a number of years it was the center of Catholic missionary activity for white settlers of the region.

## Claquato Church  1858

(originally Methodist)

CLAQUATO, LEWIS COUNTY

This is the oldest standing Protestant church in Washington. It measures approximately 20 by 30 feet and was planned from the First Methodist Church in Portland, Oregon. The belfry is a louvered square topped by a louvered octagon and surmounted by a symbolic crown of thorns.

The hill community of Claquato, a way station on the main north-south route known as Military Road between the Columbia River and Steilacoom, was founded by Lewis H. Davis. He donated land, the first lumber from his sawmill, and labor to build the church. It was deeded to the Methodist Episcopal Church on condition that it could be used by all denominations and as a school. J. D. Clinger, brother of Mrs. Lewis and an expert craftsman, supervised construction by volunteers and made the doors and casings for doors and windows himself. Settlers of the nearby town of Boisfort shaped the pews and pulpit by hand from planks.

With the coming of the railroads in the 1870s, Claquato declined in importance, but the little church continued to serve the community for many years. Although it finally fell into disrepair, it was restored in 1953 by Chehalis Post Number 22, American Legion, with financial help from the county.

## St. Paul's Episcopal Church 1865

PORT TOWNSEND, JEFFERSON COUNTY

When the church was built in 1865 it was situated on a bluff overlooking the harbor. A sea captain donated a ship's bell on condition that it be rung as a signal on foggy days. The bell guided many seamen safely to port until an official signal station was installed. The bell still rings an invitation to services each Sunday. St. Paul's is the oldest Episcopal church in the state of Washington. It has been in constant use and has been maintained in excellent condition.

The church is 20 by 42 feet. Walls are built of externally exposed vertical posts with clapboard siding between the posts. A skilled carpenter, originally from New Hampshire, who had the contract to build the church, was also a seaman, and the roof trusses seem to reflect this: the center Gothic arches combine with gracefully curved side members to give the appearance of the framing of the hull of a sailing ship. The large painted glass window over the altar was installed in 1897.

In 1883 the church was moved from the bluff to its present location a few blocks away. During the move the church was severely racked; in order to save it from collapse, the walls had to be drawn together with iron rods and clamps. These are still in place today.

## St. Paul's Catholic Church     1868

SWINOMISH INDIAN RESERVATION,
SKAGIT COUNTY

Members of the Swinomish tribe attended the first Catholic services in the area in 1840, when Father Francis Norbert Blanchet traveled from Fort Nisqually to Whidbey Island where he and the Indians erected a large wooden cross near present-day Coupeville. Later the Swinomish built their first church, a structure of poles with a roof of mats. Outside they hung a bell, which, it is said, rang the day the Point Elliot Treaty (between the United States and several Northwest Washington Indian tribes) was signed in 1855. That bell is in the present church, built under the direction of Father Casimir Chirouse, who had been appointed Indian agent for those tribes. In 1877 the church was enlarged and that same year was blessed by Bishop A. M. A. Blanchet, brother of Francis Norbert. It is located in the center of the Swinomish Tribal Community across Swinomish Channel from the town of LaConner.

Inside the church is a rare drawing of the "Catholic Ladder," devised by Father F. N. Blanchet at St. Francis Mission, near Toledo, to explain Christian and Catholic history to the Indians. Forty black horizontal bars indicate forty centuries before Christ. Thirty-three dots indicate the years of Jesus' life, followed by three crosses to mark his death. Then eighteen bars and thirty-nine dots end at the year 1839, when the ladder was first used. Among other events illustrated, including some added later, were the beginning of the world, the fall of Adam, the deluge, the Tower of Babel, the ten commandments, Jesus' birth, the twelve apostles, and the seven sacraments.

## St. Joachim's Catholic Church    1869

St. Joachim's was built on the Lummi Reservation at the time Father Casimir Chirouse served as Indian agent and missionary to Indian tribes on Puget Sound including the Muckleshoot, Suquamish, Swinomish, and Tulalip, his headquarters. Father Chirouse first visited the Lummi Reservation in 1860 and the next year, with the help of the Indians, built a little log chapel. This was replaced by the present building, which was blessed by Bishop A. M. A. Blanchet in June 1869.

In about 1920 the church was placed on skids and hauled by horses to the present location near the center of the reservation, a site donated by the Lummi's chief, Henry Kwina. In recent years the church has been reconditioned and structural reinforcements added to strengthen its walls. Inside the church are pictures of three men who were important in the early history of the church: Chief Kwina, Father Chirouse, and Father J. B. Boulet, who, after taking over the early missionary's work in 1878, continued to serve the tribe for forty years.

## St. Claire's Mission    ca. 1870

Catholic

MUCKLESHOOT INDIAN RESERVATION,
KING COUNTY

Rafters and beams of this small mission church are poles and hand-hewn timbers and the siding is hand-split cedar boards smoothed with a draw knife and secured with square-headed nails. It was built on the Muckleshoot Indian Reservation by an early-day Catholic priest with the help of several Indians and two settlers, Gilbert and Edward Courville. During the first years, missionary priests from Tulalip visited St. Claire's to conduct services for the Indians and pioneers of the area, which included present-day Auburn, Buckley, and Enumclaw.

High winds damaged the building in 1934 and, although later repaired by local Indians, it fell into disuse and was abandoned. In the early 1960s it was moved to a site in Federal Way for historic preservation purposes. In 1979, however, it was moved back to the Muckleshoot Indian Reservation for restoration and use by members of the tribe. St. Claire's is a good example of an early building constructed where milled wood was not available. The photograph to the right was taken at the Federal Way location.

## St. Paul's Episcopal Church    1870
(originally Congregational)

PORT GAMBLE, KITSAP COUNTY

The First Congregational Church of East Machias, Maine, the home of the Pope and Talbot families who founded the town of Port Gamble, is the model for this fine church. It is a splendid example of early New England architecture, richly enhanced with fine detail, and is outstanding among the earliest churches of Washington State. The church is set back slightly from the tree-lined road, its yard enclosed by a white picket fence.

The divided pews, which are numbered, are also copied from the church in Maine. There, following New England tradition, pews were sold or rented to raise money for the church. It was the custom in the 1800s for all the members of a family to sit together in "their" pew. Divided slip pews were a modification of the earlier box pews, which had high side walls and a door at the end.

Port Gamble was established in 1853 as a company mill town. Houses, stores, offices, a hotel as well as the church were built by the company. The church bell was a gift from wives of company officials in San Francisco.

In 1870, the year the church was built, *Overland Monthly* included in a survey of the lumber industry: ". . . the Port Gamble Mill cuts a greater amount, employs more hands, and is by far the most extensive establishment of the kind in the Territory, being known under the name of Puget Mill Company. Two hundred men are employed about the mill, and the same number in the logging camps. . . ."

The Pope and Talbot Company maintains the church today.

## Unitarian Meeting House    1872
(originally Methodist)

TUMWATER, THURSTON COUNTY

This small frame church stands on the hillside a short distance from the falls of the Deschutes River, where, in 1845, Michael T. Simmons founded the first American settlement on Puget Sound, naming it New Market. Later the name was changed to Tumwater. Simmons built a flour mill and a sawmill, both of which he sold in 1850 to Captain Clanrick Crosby, a sea captain from the East Coast who came to the Pacific to trade during the California gold rush. Crosby and Nelson Barnes, a mill owner who came to Tumwater in 1852, were largely responsible for completion of the church debt free.

Methodist circuit riders had served the area for several years. After a series of revival meetings, citizens of the town decided to build a community church. Barnes, a Methodist, donated the land. Crosby made a challenge: "I will give as much as my friend Barnes." In one day thirteen hundred dollars was raised. Labor and materials were also donated. The church, completed in 1872, was used for a time by Presbyterians, Unitarians, and Episcopalians.

Some additions have been made in later years, but the building remains much the same as when originally built. The unusual sharply pointed pediment over the door, the small round window above, and the classic detailing of the belfry are its only ornamentation.

## St. Peter's Chapel-at-Ease    1873

Episcopal

TACOMA, PIERCE COUNTY

Tacoma's oldest church opened on August 10, 1873. It was quickly built after the announcement on July 15 that Tacoma had been named the western terminus of the Northern Pacific Railroad. The first line connected Tacoma with Kalama on the Columbia River.

George E. Atkinson, church member and superintendent of a sawmill, managed the rapid construction of the 21-by-45-foot building. Rough sawn boards and battens were used on the exterior walls, and the bell tower was a cedar tree cut to a 40-foot height and topped by a small belfry. The bell was donated by the Sunday school of St. Peter's Church of Philadelphia in 1874. The interior, which is essentially in the original condition, has walls and ceiling of white-painted grooved boards, hanging lanterns, the old pews, a pot-belly stove, and a pump organ.

In the early years of the church, Episcopalians shared their building with Catholic and many Protestant groups needing a meeting place.

## The Valley Church  1882
(originally Presbyterian)

SAN JUAN ISLAND, SAN JUAN COUNTY

The cornerstone shows the date 1878, but it was not until four years later that the church was completed. It is a traditional frame church with the entrance enclosure and steeple at one corner. The Gothic windows, with their edges bordered by small panes of clear red, blue, green, and yellow glass, are unusually attractive. The site for the church was donated by R. M. Lundblad, who is buried in the adjoining cemetery. The majority of the first members were English, Scottish, and Scandinavian. A tradition at Christmas time was to set up a large tree, under which families would place a package for each of their children. At the time of carol singing during the Christmas service the packages were distributed.

The church is in a rural area near the American camp where soldiers were stationed during the "Pig War" of the 1850s, before the official boundary treaty of 1872 made San Juan Island a part of the United States. The following year Washington's territorial legislature established San Juan County.

The church is open now for special services such as weddings and funerals.

## Avon United Methodist Church 1884

AVON, SKAGIT COUNTY

In 1877, after great effort, the huge log jams that blocked the Skagit River near its mouth were broken, opening the upper river to steamboat travel. Logging companies quickly moved in to cut timber, and homesteaders took up claims and cleared land for farms. A number of settlers, many of English and Scottish heritage, took up land north of Mount Vernon. Arthur H. Skaling opened a store and founded a "no-saloons" town on the river bend, naming it Avon in honor of the birthplace of William Shakespeare. Soon the town had a post office, shingle mill, boat works, and additional stores. Avon claimed a population of five hundred.

In 1884 a Methodist church was organized with twenty-one charter members. Skaling, whose ancestors in England were friends of John Wesley, donated the land and drew the plans for a church building. Money, labor, and materials were also donated and the edifice, which at first had only animal skins covering window openings, was put into immediate use. It was completed and dedicated in 1887, debt free. Originally near the river bank, the church was moved a short distance to its present site in 1920.

Although the basic design is simple, there are a number of fine architectural details, including the ornamental gables and fancy-cut shingles of the steeple, the quatrefoil pattern in the round window above the entrance, and the pediments over the Gothic-shaped main windows.

38

## Bayview United Methodist Church    1888

BAYVIEW, SKAGIT COUNTY

Bayview, situated on a wooded ridge at the edge of Padilla Bay, was founded in 1884. A short time before, a merchant from California had bought an acre of land here and opened a general store to provide supplies for loggers and mill workers in the heavily timbered area and for the farmers clearing and diking the nearby lowlands. A town of two blocks was platted, consisting of a few houses, a general store, a hotel, a saloon, a sawmill, a shingle mill, and a post office that distributed mail brought from LaConner once a week.

In 1888 the founders of the town helped organize a Methodist church, and a building was constructed that same year. The L-shaped structure follows a standard design of the Methodist Extension Society. The vestibule of the bell tower has two interior doors—one to the sanctuary of the church, the other to a room that can be used for Sunday school or social activities or opened to the sanctuary to accommodate a larger congregation. Few changes have been made on the interior, and the exterior also remains in almost original condition.

The exterior design has some interesting architectural details, including the trefoil and quatrefoil cutouts in the bargeboards at the gable ends. The quatrefoil shapes there are repeated in the large round windows and in the pediments over the rectangular windows. The belfry is also attractively detailed with turning lathe and scroll saw parts.

## St. Mary's Catholic Church    1889
(originally Congregational)

COUPEVILLE, ISLAND COUNTY

In the fall of 1886 Congregationalists opened Puget Sound Academy in Coupeville to provide higher education for boys and girls. For many years the school attracted students from a wide area around the Sound.

The church, which the Congregationalists built in 1889 next to Puget Sound Academy and used until 1930, was purchased by the Archdiocese of Seattle in 1934 and became St. Mary's Catholic Church. It was recently refurbished in an unusually interesting way. After considerable research to determine the original color scheme, the church was repainted in those same colors—brown, yellow, and white—which were used when it was first completed.

Although the basic design of the church is similar to New England Congregational church architecture, the builders added many decorative Victorian details, including fancy-cut shingles, boards laid in herringbone patterns, sunburst panels, and half-circle louvers. The large stained-glass windows are also particularly impressive. Simple geometric patterns are repeated, but each is different because of the great variation in the color and value of the individual panes.

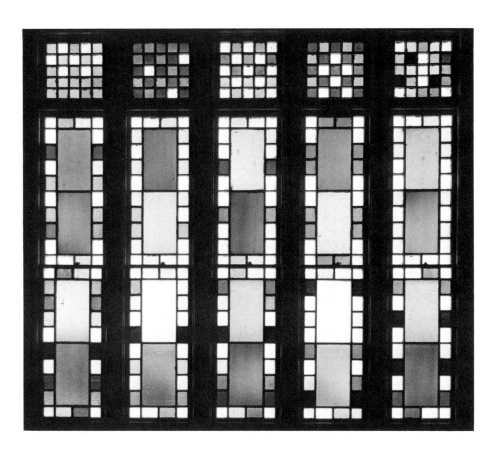

## *Willapa United Methodist Church* 1889

WILLAPA, PACIFIC COUNTY

Beginning in the 1850s a trading post at the site of Willapa provided supplies to settlers and to travelers using the coastal route and river valleys on their journey to Puget Sound. By the 1880s Willapa was a boom town with two real estate offices, three hotels, and three blacksmith shops. It was the supply point for several logging camps in the area, and people there expected a railroad boom.

In 1886 land was donated for a Methodist church. Donations to the building fund included $250 from the Methodist Extension Society in the East. The 28-by-47-foot building followed a standard plan furnished by the extension society and cost $1,405. The pastor at the time the church was built wrote: "S. D. Stearns the carpenter made ready the seats, windows and door frames, during the winter. The windows, doors and mouldings were on the ground early in the spring and paid for. The building was ready for occupancy July 20th when we held our last quarterly meeting in it. . . . We placed in the tower a 400 pound Bell of Pure Bell Mettle. From the McShane Bell Foundery, Baltimore, Md."

In 1893 the Northern Pacific branch line was completed to South Bend, bypassing Willapa. Hotel keepers and businessmen soon moved away and the town quickly lost its business and trade to Raymond and South Bend. The town never regained its former importance.

## First United Presbyterian Church   1890

PORT TOWNSEND, JEFFERSON COUNTY

In 1872 the Board of Home Missions of the Presbyterian Church sent a minister from Pennsylvania to Port Townsend. The next year a church was organized with seven women as charter members, and plans were soon made to build a church. A lot was purchased for $250 in gold. In 1875 work began on a stone church, with donations of money, materials, and labor. Adults and children from the whole community help to haul stone from the surrounding hillsides and open areas. Dedicated two years later, it was the first stone church erected in the territory.

During the years of railroad expansion in the 1880s, many fine buildings were erected in Port Townsend in expectation of a great growth in population. The Presbyterians decided to replace their small stone church with the present large handsome frame church, using the stone from the first for the foundation of the new. Construction began in 1889 and the church was completed the next year at a cost of almost twenty thousand dollars. The impressive interior includes the pipes of a tracker organ, large exposed roof truss beams, natural wood paneling, curved pews (seating six hundred), and beautiful stained-glass windows. The church was designed by Port Townsend architects William T. Whiteway and Julius C. Schroeder.

Shortly after the completion of the church the boom in Port Townsend collapsed. The church was in severe financial straits for several years but managed to survive, and in later years many improvements and additions were made.

46

*New Age Christian Church*    1890
(originally German Congregational)

SEATTLE, KING COUNTY

This small frame church is in Ballard, a neighborhood in the northwest part of Seattle. Ballard began as a mill town and was incorporated in 1890, the year the church was built by a recently organized congregation led by Pastor Gottlieb Graedel, a missionary who traveled throughout the Northwest seeking German settlers. The church was active for about ten years but finally closed for lack of support. For a short time the building was rented to the Ballard School Board to house a school.

Then in 1904, when Ballard had grown from a tiny village to a community of ten thousand with twelve lumber and shingle mills and an active fishing fleet, the recently organized St. Paul's Evangelical Church, another German congregation led by the Reverend E. Leutwein, rented the building briefly before purchasing it for five hundred dollars, enough to satisfy the outstanding mortgage. Immediately volunteers began extensive remodeling and repairs. The original tall steeple, which had become unsafe, was replaced. Fancy-cut shingles on the belfry and gable end and a variety of shapes in window and louver openings show an attempt to increase the ornamentation of the basic, simply designed structure. This church is a fine example of many of the early-day churches built by small congregations in the Northwest.

## Little White Church on the Hill  1890

Lutheran

SILVANA, SNOHOMISH COUNTY

This is one of several Lutheran churches in the area that were built by Scandinavians who came from their homeland in large numbers during the 1880s. This congregation was founded in 1884 under the leadership of the Reverend Christian Jorgenson from the Stanwood Lutheran church. That same year land was purchased for a church and cemetery on a hill above the banks of the Stillaguamish River overlooking the rich delta farm land. Transporting building materials to the site was difficult. Lumber purchased at the Utsalady mill was towed on scows to Stanwood and then upriver as far as possible. During the cold winter of 1890, thick ice on the river and a cover of snow made it possible for the lumber to be hauled on large sleds drawn by oxen across the river and up the hill to the building site. The cost of materials was $750; all members helped in the construction, donating their labor. The first service was held on Christmas, 1890, before the church was completely finished.

The Ladies Aid and the Young People's Society helped raise funds to complete the interior and decorate it, but it was not until 1897 that the chancel rail and altar were installed. The steeple was also added at a later date.

## Epworth Chapel 1890

Methodist

STANWOOD, SNOHOMISH COUNTY

Fancy-cut shingles and wood trim ornament this 30-by-50-foot building, which followed Methodist Extension Society Plan 28. When first built the exterior was painted in several colors, accenting the various patterns of the shingles and architectural details. Color was also used in the tall, narrow, pointed windows, a variety of pastel hues in the individual panes. Kerosene lamps and an elaborate chandelier lighted the church until 1929. The chandelier, pictured below, now hangs in the present Methodist church across the street.

Methodist preaching began here in 1877 in homes or in the schoolhouse. In 1884 a church was organized with twelve members. D. O. Pearson, one of the board members, had come to the area in 1877. He was born in Lowell, Massachusetts, and in 1866, at age twenty, came with the second group of New Englanders brought to the Northwest by Asa Mercer. Pearson joined other members of his family on Whidbey Island where he was a farmer before moving to Stanwood, at that time called Centerville. He gave the town the new name Stanwood after the maiden name of his wife, who also came from Massachusetts.

## Montesano United Methodist Church 1891

MONTESANO, GRAYS HARBOR COUNTY

In 1852 the first settlers to this area came from Maine by ship around Cape Horn to San Francisco, then up the coast to Washington, finally selecting a site on the south bank of the Chehalis River for their donation land claim. The settlement, first called Scammon, was named for the founder. His wife, a very religious person, wanted the name changed to Mount Zion, but compromised with Montesano, which sounded more pleasant and had about the same meaning. A Methodist circuit rider visited the community in 1859 and a congregation was organized the next year. A church was built in 1885.

However, a new town, also called Montesano, was platted in a more desirable location about a mile and a half upstream and across the river from the first town, and most new settlers and businesses preferred the new site. In 1886 the county seat was moved to this location and in 1891 the Methodists built a new church, the present building.

One of the most interesting features of the interior of this large frame church is the system of large exposed roof trusses that crisscross the ceiling diagonally and span the gable ends. The dark-stained truss members, which have decorative carving and quatrefoil cutouts, form a striking pattern against the light-colored ceiling. The church exterior also includes interesting decorative effects in the millwork and scrollwork of the belfry and gable ends.

## Orting United Methodist Church    1891

ORTING, PIERCE COUNTY

Orting is one of the farming communities in the flat river valley of the Puyallup homesteaded by Kansas farmers who had struggled across Naches Pass in 1852. Methodist circuit riders first came to the valley in 1857. Twenty years later Methodists began preaching at Orting in a small log hut that was also used as a schoolhouse. In 1890 lots were acquired, some purchased and some donated, and money was borrowed from the Board of Missions to build the present church. Completed in 1891, the church has been in service ever since. It was closed only once, in 1906, during a scarlet fever epidemic. The church has been enlarged three times as membership increased.

A variety of fancy-cut shingles were used for the exterior siding, resulting in a highly textured decorative exterior.

## Oysterville Church 1892

(originally Baptist)

Beginning in 1851 sailing ships came to Shoal-water Bay (now Willapa Bay) to pick up cargoes of piling, timber, and oysters, all much in demand at San Francisco. In 1854 I. A. Clark, a tailor from New York, and R. H. Espy, a lumberman from Wisconsin, hearing of good oystering grounds at the north tip of Long Beach Peninsula, took out donation land claims there. Clark platted a town near the oystering grounds, naming it Oysterville.

The town grew and prospered as other oystermen and their families settled there, and it was the county seat from 1855 to 1893. In 1863 it had its own public schoolhouse.

Baptist ministers began visiting the town in 1871 but it was not until 1892, a time of great Baptist missionary zeal in the Northwest, that a church of that denomination was built at Oysterville. It was constructed at a cost of fifteen hundred dollars by pioneer settler R. H. Espy. The church (which now belongs to the Espy family), a few houses, and the schoolhouse are all that remain of the old town today.

## Our Lady of Good Voyage Chapel  1892

Catholic (originally Methodist)

ROCHE HARBOR, SAN JUAN COUNTY

Roche Harbor was the site of a Hudson's Bay Company operation, a lime processing plant, which began on San Juan Island in the 1850s. In 1886 the plant was taken over by John S. McMillin, who made the lime operation the largest west of the Mississippi. *Coast Magazine* reported in 1904 that the company town included kilns, warehouses, a large hotel, houses, and a school and church—all painted white. The church, originally built for a schoolhouse, was used by Methodists for Sunday afternoon services. After a decline in the lime business, the church stood empty for many years. It was beautifully renovated by Mrs. Clara Tarte after the Tarte family purchased the village in 1956 and Roche Harbor became a pleasure-boat haven. The furnishings were donated from other old parishes: the altar from Holy Family Church, Kirkland, and the pews from Holy Family Church, White Center. In 1960 it was blessed as a Catholic chapel.

*Coupeville United Methodist Church*   1894

COUPEVILLE, ISLAND COUNTY

This fine frame church, which rests on a stone foundation, is painted gray with white trim accenting the interesting architectural features and details. The bell tower, with its turrets and steeple, stands at a corner of the building.

In 1853 the first Methodist preachers came to Ebey's Landing on Whidbey Island, holding services in pioneer settlers' homes. The first church was built in 1859. In 1885 a new building was erected at the present site but burned in 1893, unfortunately a few days after the insurance had lapsed. In spite of this and the financial depression at that time, a new structure, the present church, was started that year and completed in 1894. It was built by Howard B. Lovejoy, who also built a number of houses in the community. Numerous additions and changes have been made to the church over the years. In 1960, after seeking professional counsel, the congregation decided to retain the old sanctuary because of its historical value and architectural merit and it was subsequently restored.

Whidbey Island was settled early. Among the first to come was Captain Thomas Coupe, who took up a claim in 1852 at Penn Cove, the site of the town of Coupeville. He was from New England, as were many of the early settlers, and their influence remains in the town to this day.

## St. John's Episcopal Church    1894

SNOHOMISH, SNOHOMISH COUNTY

As early as 1860 there was a trading post on the banks of the Snohomish River at the site of Snohomish. When the town was first established it was dependent upon steamboat transportation, but in the late 1880s the Seattle, Lakeshore and Eastern Railroad came north from Seattle. This lumber and agricultural town continued to grow when other railroads came through the valley, and many immigrants came to work in the forests, mills, and farms of the area.

The first Episcopal services were held in Snohomish in 1889, and for the next ten years the officiating clergyman, the Reverend C. J. Brenton, came from Victoria each week by steamer. In the fall of 1893, property was purchased and a contract was signed to build the church for $250; this small sum was possible because most of the materials were donated by the members. The design was from a New England church. Construction was slowed because of the great financial panic of 1893, but in 1894 St. John's was completed and has been in continuous use since. Although the church is now crowded in by other buildings, the belfry with its fine wood details can easily be seen from many parts of the town. A number of beautiful stained-glass windows have been added over the years.

The church has served not only the people of Snohomish but also those as far away as Gold Bar to the east and Arlington to the north.

*Our Lady of Lourdes*
*Catholic Church*   1894

WILKESON, PIERCE COUNTY

This small white church, with its square belfry, octagonal steeple, and bright red door, is about two blocks from the center of town. Originally built high on a hillside, it was moved in recent times to the present site on the banks of Wilkeson Creek where it is now more easily reached.

Coal had been discovered in the Wilkeson area at an early date, but mining operations did not start until 1876 when the Northern Pacific Railroad built a branch line from Tacoma. After agitation over Chinese labor began in 1885, many southern and eastern Europeans were recruited to work in the mines and forests.

Catholic priests visited Wilkeson beginning in the late 1880s. In 1892 Father Michael Fafara, a Polish priest ordained in Rome, arrived in Washington State to work among the recent Slavic immigrants. From Tacoma, his headquarters, he visited many small towns and groups. He came to Wilkeson by horse and buggy once a month, conducting Mass in a schoolhouse. In 1893 Peter Chromoga and John Pete gave land for a church, which was completed and blessed the next year. In 1905 the growing congregation purchased land for a Catholic cemetery.

Strikes and labor disturbances after 1912 caused a dramatic drop in population in the mining area.

*Eagle Harbor*
*Congregational Church*    1896
United Church of Christ
WINSLOW, KITSAP COUNTY

A group of pioneers in the community, mostly of Scots-Irish, German, and Scandinavian descent, met in 1881 to organize a church. Like some other early churches, the denomination was determined by compromise, as indicated in the church records: "The citizens of Eagle Harbor Settlement, being of several different organizations, it was mutually agreed by them to unite, in some form of church government which was least objectionable, and the Congregational form was agreed upon."

An acre of land was donated by Ambrose Grow and his wife, who were charter members; money covering the cost of the church, $1,050, was raised by donations, suppers, quiltings, and bazaars before the church was built. Members chose the design of a standard New England Congregational church with an open belfry and large rectangular windows. Materials were from the nearby Port Blakely and Port Madison mills and were brought to Eagle Harbor by sailing sloop. Large timbers for the church were hand hewn by John Parfitt, a charter member, and hauled to the building site by oxen.

The fine craftsmanship in the structure, shingle trim, and architectural details of the church reflects the high skill level of the craftsmen and carpenters of the vast shipbuilding industry of the community at that time.

## Vaughn Community Church 1897

(originally Episcopal)

VAUGHN, PIERCE COUNTY

The Reverend Leigh W. Applegate, an Episcopal archdeacon, purchased property on a beautiful small peninsula on Vaughn Bay and supplied materials from his nearby sawmill for this church. Labor was donated by local residents. The interior, in excellent and original condition, is unusual—dark exposed crossbeams with side walls in patterns of brown- and green-stained shingles.

For a short time the Episcopalians shared their building on alternate Sundays with a Presbyterian congregation that had met for four years at the town's library. After Mr. Applegate's mill burned and he left the area, the Presbyterians bought the church. Their minister, the Reverend Thomas Weekes, served several congregations. For twelve years he came by steamboat on alternate Sundays, preaching at Vaughn in the morning and Allyn in the evening. As in the case of many other churches built along the waterways of the Pacific Northwest, some members also came by small water craft to attend church services and functions.

In later years the church, which became known as "The Chapel by the Sea," has been served by ministers of several other denominations including Congregational, Christian, Baptist, and now Village Missions.

## Sacred Heart Catholic Church    1899

LACONNER, SKAGIT COUNTY

LaConner began in 1867 as a trading post named Swinomish, located on the east side of the channel and across from the Swinomish Indian Reservation. In 1869 John S. Conner purchased the post and later changed the name to LaConner in honor of his wife Louisa A.—her initials forming the prefix to the name. LaConner prospered and became a regular port of call for steamboats traveling weekly between Seattle and Whatcom. Beginning in 1871, Mrs. Conner, a devout Catholic, successfully raised money for a church which was built during the next year by Father F. X. Prefontaine, who served as architect, builder, and painter. It stood on the hill overlooking the channel.

In 1899 the present church was built in a new location. A newspaper reported: ". . . the most important of the new structures now going up is the large Catholic church edifice that will add beauty and dignity to the public buildings of our town. The dimensions of this new church are 40×85 feet, with a class and vestry room at the rear 14×16 feet each. When completed it will cost over $3,000 and will be capable of seating 500 persons. . . ."

The twin steeples of the church can be seen from many points as one approaches the town. Other interesting features are the apse, the large rose window in the front, and the repeat of the Gothic window shapes in bell tower and belfry. Beautiful stained-glass windows were added in 1902. Exterior and interior remain in fine original condition.

## First Congregational Church    ca. 1900
### United Church of Christ
FOX ISLAND, PIERCE COUNTY

The church at Sylvan on Fox Island, like some other churches in small communities along Puget Sound, stands close to the shore of a quiet bay. It is interesting to note that the belfry is located on the end of the church nearest the water. The church, organized in 1892, was built at the turn of the century when waterways were still the main highways for Northwest travelers in areas not served by railroads. More than one minister traveled his circuit by steamboat, stopping briefly to conduct a service, then continuing on by boat to another landing to preach to another congregation later in the day.

Sylvan, on the Hale Passage side of the island, was founded in 1888 by A. J. Miller, who helped organize the Congregational church a few years later. He had bought a large tract of land and sold parcels of it to relatives and friends who came from his former home in central Iowa. *The Bay Island Country,* a booklet published in 1912, told of the opportunities and attributes of communities in the area. Sylvan, it reported, "is noted for its pretty homes, apples, strawberries. . . . The village has one store, post office, good school, church, public library and a historical society. There are two steamers daily to Tacoma, making daily mail service, in addition to launch service which connects with trolley line from Tacoma at Higgins Beach, making hourly trips during the day and special trips at night for theater parties."

*Holy Trinity Orthodox Church*     1900

WILKESON, PIERCE COUNTY

Holy Trinity, the oldest Orthodox church in Washington, was built at the turn of the century shortly after many Slavic immigrants came to the area to work in the coal mines. The tiny church is similar to the churches built by Russians in Alaska before it was sold to the United States in 1867. Topping the octagonal belfry is a blue "onion dome" surmounted by the golden three-barred Slavic cross. The Gothic-shaped multipaned windows, the cross and icon on the gabled porch, and the fancy-cut brackets on porch and belfry are particularly interesting exterior features.

The interior walls and ceiling are narrow boards painted white. A screen called an *ikonostas,* on which icons are placed, separates the sanctuary from the main body of the church. There is no formal seating in the church because most worshipers stand to offer services with the priest.

Coal mining declined in Wilkeson beginning in 1912. Later the church was abandoned and fell into disrepair. Andrew and Anna Michal, who moved to nearby South Prairie in 1929, gradually restored it at their own expense. The church today is in excellent condition.

## Chinook Evangelical Lutheran Church 1901

CHINOOK, PACIFIC COUNTY

The town of Chinook is located on the east shore of Baker Bay near the mouth of the Columbia, just downstream from the site of the early Indian village of the same name. The area was first visited by white men in 1792 when Captain Robert Gray, a sea trader from Boston, brought his sailing ship through the heavy surf, crossed the hazardous bar, and entered the river. He named the great river after his ship *Columbia.*

The present town became an established fishing community in the late 1870s; fish traps located there required large investment and a stable population. Some of the people who came were American-born, but a great many were Scandinavian sailors and fishermen who came to work in the salmon fishery.

In 1899 wives of fishermen, who had growing families, organized a Ladies Aid society to press for a Lutheran church for their small community. The church, designed by a carpenter from Astoria, Oregon, was built with volunteer labor and financed by local subscription. It served a congregation of Swedes, Norwegians, and Danes.

*Deep River*
*Pioneer Lutheran Church*   1902

DEEP RIVER, WAHKIAKUM COUNTY

This small church stands on a road that winds along the narrow valley of the Deep River, one of the many small rivers in this region that empty into the Columbia. It was built by Finnish immigrants who began settling here in the early 1880s. The simple design is enhanced by the darker color of the trim and corner boards and the diamond-shaped shingles of the belfry and steeple. The rather austere interior is relieved somewhat by the diagonal pattern of the narrow boards on the walls. The painting above the simple altar was done by the first pastor of the church.

Finnish seamen first visited the Columbia River on English and Russian sailing vessels that came for the fur or timber trade or for fishing or whaling. When the salmon industry grew along the Columbia, many of these single men became fishermen, turning to the logging industry in the winter months when there was no fishing. Their letters home and to the Great Lakes region attracted many more of their countrymen. Many settled on recently logged-off land, clearing and draining their claims to establish farms and dairies while working at other jobs.

The Finns were eager to provide secular and religious education for their children, and there was a need for social activity. They established lodges and churches to fulfill these needs.

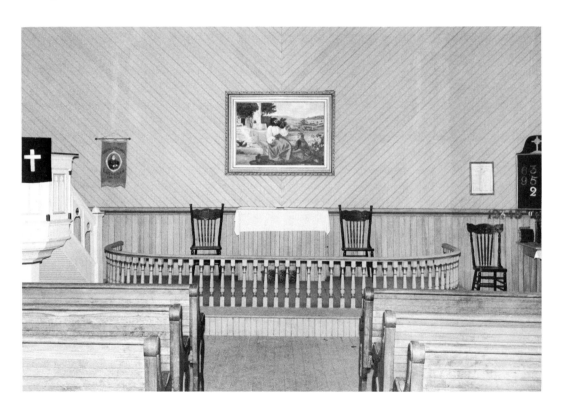

## Calvary Lutheran Church    1902

EVERETT, SNOHOMISH COUNTY

In 1901 a group of Norwegian Lutherans in Everett organized the Zion Lutheran Free Church and in 1902 built a church and parsonage. The design utilizes the corner lot effectively with the corner steeple and entrance placed at an angle. The steeple is ornamented only by a wooden cross on its front face, gables at the base of the tall octagonal spire, and a simple finial at the top. The rectangular plan of the church is broken on its long side by a slightly projecting gable. Within this gable is a large Gothic window identical to the window at the end of the church.

The founding of Everett as a deliberately selected and planned community on Puget Sound contrasts sharply with the beginnings of most other towns in Washington State, which had their origins as trading posts, early settlements, or railroad junctions. In 1891 land developers, lumber men, industrialists, railroad builders, and capitalists joined together to build an industrial city at the mouth of the Snohomish River. Everett, advertised as "Pittsburgh of the Pacific Coast," was platted with a central business and residential district and with mills, factories, smelters, shipyards, and railyards along the river, tideflats, and Sound. Building and expansion were rapid but suffered a stunning setback during the Panic of 1893 when many eastern capitalists withdrew their support. Growth resumed, however, at the turn of the century when the Weyerhauser Timber Company began construction of a new mill, the largest in the world.

82

## Preston Baptist Church    1902

PRESTON, KING COUNTY

In 1888 a group of Swedish Baptists came to Washington from Minnesota to work in lumber camps and mills near Snoqualmie Pass. In 1892 they bought a shingle mill near Preston which, after a few difficult years caused by the Panic of 1893, began to flourish under the leadership of August Lovegren, one of the original owners. Later a new shingle mill and sawmill were built in Preston and attracted large numbers of Swedish Baptist immigrants, some of whom came directly from Sweden and Finland.

In March 1900 twelve people, including Lovegren, organized the Swedish Baptist Assembly, and twenty others soon transferred their membership from Seattle, Ballard, and Tacoma. The company donated a 40-by-180-foot lot in the mill yard, and in 1902 the present church was built. Although the original cost estimate was seven hundred dollars, a higher bell tower, larger front windows, and "ingrained" wallpaper instead of painted walls in the sanctuary increased the cost to one thousand dollars. Their first pastor received an annual salary of two hundred dollars. Traditions of the church that date from the earliest times include the New Year's Watchnight service, the Offerfest of Thanksgiving, the 6:00 A.M. Julotto (Christmas services), and church picnics.

## St. Peter's Catholic Church    1902

SUQUAMISH, KITSAP COUNTY

The first church erected by the Suquamish Indians was dedicated as St. Peter's in 1871 by Bishop A. M. A. Blanchet. It was dismantled in 1902 after the United States government requested that site for inclusion in a military reserve. The present church was built at a new location on the Port Madison Indian Reservation. Doors and windows of the original building were saved and used in the new building. Lumber was ferried across Agate Pass by rowboat. The simple design is ornamented by a four-sided cupola with round arch louvered openings and topped by a wooden cross.

The church stands next to the Suquamish Memorial Cemetery, burial place of Chief Sealth, who died in 1866. He was a great friend of early white settlers, who named Seattle in his honor. The small white stone cross, seen through the lower left part of the church window in the photograph, marks his grave.

## Camano Lutheran Church    1904

CAMANO ISLAND, ISLAND COUNTY

In 1891, in the town of Utsalady on Camano Island, a Norwegian Lutheran congregation was chartered and a site chosen for a church. But the large sawmill there closed and many of the families moved elsewhere. Some of the people moved to nearby Livingston Bay, where services were held in a schoolhouse. In 1895 the minister, who also served at Stanwood, was paid a yearly salary of fifty-one dollars for his work at Livingston Bay.

The present site was donated in 1900 and in 1904 money was raised to build a church. Many members worked to complete the building, which was dedicated in 1906. The exterior has been changed, principally by extensive additions, but the old church interior is much the same as the original. The pulpit, baptismal font, and a beautiful altar were carved and inlaid by some of the early members, who used "old country" skills and hand tools to create these pieces in a nearby carpenter's shop. Eleven kinds of wood were used, given to the craftsmen by captains of sailing ships that came to the large steam sawmill at Utsalady to pick up lumber for shipment to ports around the world. Inscribed on the altar is the biblical phrase in Norwegian, "Kommer hid til mig, Alle" ("Come unto me, all"). There is also a finely detailed painted wood screen at ceiling height separating the chancel from the rest of the church. The screen, of scroll work and turned parts, reflects the traditional wood crafts of Scandinavia.

*Holy Family Catholic Church*     1904

FRANCES, PACIFIC COUNTY

In 1887 several Swiss-Germans homesteaded in the heavily timbered area near the border of Lewis County in the Willapa River valley. In 1890 the Northern Pacific Railroad began building a branch line from Chehalis Junction to the coast, and during the next twenty years many Swiss, Germans, and Poles moved into the area. In 1893 a town was platted at the railway station, which had been named Frances after the wife of an official of the railway.

Catholic priests began visiting the area, saying Mass at private homes. In 1900 a small church was built in Frances just below the Catholic cemetery on the hillside. In 1904 the church was enlarged and completed under the direction of Father Severinus Jurek, a Dominican priest who was pastor in Pe Ell. Frances became the headquarters of Catholic parishes in Pacific County. In 1908 a parochial school opened, its teachers Benedictine sisters from Missouri.

The design of the church is unusual. Two doors flank the main entrance, reminiscent of the large churches and cathedrals of central Europe. The church interior is richly ornamented with large paintings from Switzerland, carved altars that were made by one of the members, and the painted glass windows at either side of the main altar.

## St. Mary's Catholic Church  1904

MCGOWAN, PACIFIC COUNTY

A few miles upstream from the town of Chinook, near the banks of the Columbia, stands the weathered gray Catholic church at McGowan. A short distance away is the site of the Chinook Indian village, famous in the early 1800s for its salmon fishery. The Hudson's Bay Company opened a post at the Chinook village in 1840, the same year the Catholic missionary Modeste Demers visited there. Demers was followed eight years later by Father Louis Leonette, who established a mission at the village.

In 1853 Patrick J. McGowan, an Irish businessman from Portland, bought the 320-acre mission site and in a few years established salmon-packing plants there. In 1904 McGowan erected the present church on the former mission site at a cost of thirty-five hundred dollars. He presented the church and property to the Catholic Archdiocese and it was dedicated as St. Mary's two years later. For many years Mass was held there once a month for the few Irish families who lived near the church. After the neighboring canneries closed, the church was seldom used, and the building was neglected until 1961 when restoration work began. Now the church is in excellent condition; the interior is much the same as it was when it was built. Mass is offered during the summer months.

## St. Anne's Catholic Church    1904

TULALIP INDIAN RESERVATION,
SNOHOMISH COUNTY

St. Anne's stands on a gently sloping hill overlooking Tulalip Bay. It is an exceptionally fine frame church with many interesting architectural details, including the ogee arch portal of the bell tower. Handsome wrought-iron hinges accent the door, over which are the words "St. Anne, Pray For Us." The church was built to replace the original St. Anne's, built in 1861 and destroyed by fire in 1902.

In 1857, after the Indian peace treaty was signed, Father Casimir Chirouse established a mission at Tulalip and founded a school for Indian children. Father Chirouse was one of the Oblate priests from France whose mission there was to preach and work among the poor. In the 1840s a number of Oblates were sent to Canada and the Pacific Northwest to work among the Indians and the few Europeans here. Their assignment was to build schools, churches, and convents; they served as architects, carpenters, painters, and laborers. Most of those who came to Washington Territory were transferred to British Columbia in 1858. Father Chirouse remained at Tulalip for twenty more years, living and working with the Indians. When he joined the other Oblates in Canada in 1878, his work was continued by Father J. B. Boulet, a secular priest.

## Church of St. Anne    1905
Catholic

This unpretentious white frame church was built by Father J. B. Boulet, who used his own savings for its construction. The two lots of the churchyard were provided by local Catholics. Boulet, a teacher from Quebec, came to Washington Territory in 1864 to work among the Indians. He helped rebuild St. Joseph's Mission at Tampico and in 1878, after he was ordained, took over Father Casimir Chirouse's Puget Sound Indian district, which included the Lummi tribe of Whatcom County. In 1889 he was sent to Whatcom (Bellingham) where, as priest to both Indians and white people, he looked after two churches and eighteen missions. He was much loved and respected by all who knew him.

In addition to his many priestly duties, Boulet had earlier been a writer and publisher, printing on his own press many of his works, among them, in 1879, a prayer book and catechism in the Skagit language. Between 1882 and 1887, while stationed at Puyallup, he published a juvenile monthly magazine *The Youths' Companion,* with stories for Indian children, prayers, and letters from priests and nuns. Money derived from its circulation of fifteen hundred, including many subscribers in the East, permitted the building of a number of Puget Sound area Indian churches.

## Chinook United Methodist Church    1906

CHINOOK, PACIFIC COUNTY

In 1894 a Methodist evangelist visited Chinook and a number of people were converted as a result of his revival meetings. In 1896 a church was organized and that same year a church building was erected at a cost of four hundred dollars. The land was donated by H. S. Gile and his wife Matilda, daughter of one of the early settlers of Oysterville.

The first building was replaced in 1906 by the present building on the same site. Interesting design features of this simple frame church include the dark-shingled octagonal steeple and the large window at the front. This window is Gothic in style but has angular rather than curved members at the top, probably to make construction easier.

## Elbe Lutheran Church   1906

ELBE, PIERCE COUNTY

Immigrants from the Elbe River country near Hamburg, Germany, homesteaded this forested area on the banks of the Nisqually River near Mount Rainier. Beginning in 1893, Lutheran ministers came from Tacoma or Puyallup once a month to conduct Sunday afternoon worship services and to perform other rites in the German language.

In 1906 Pastor Karl Killian of Puyallup drew plans for this tiny church, which is only 18 by 24 feet. Henry Lutkens, founder of Elbe, donated the building site and lumber. Labor was also donated. The tall steeple holds a bell and is topped by an iron cross made by the town blacksmith.

Pastor Killian was not only church designer, preacher, and teacher but also the church organist, playing on the small reed organ that is still in place. To come to Elbe from Puyallup, he rode his bicycle to the Long Line Streetcar, which he boarded for Tacoma, taking his bicycle with him. He then transferred to the Tacoma and Eastern Railway to Elbe. There he once again used his bicycle or borrowed a horse and buggy to visit church members.

*First Lutheran Church*     1908

POULSBO, KITSAP COUNTY

The church stands on a hill, overlooking the town, the bay, and the shoreline. The tall steeple, with its many gables and pinnacles, reminds one of the ornate "stave" churches of Norway.

In 1886 a group of recent Norwegian immigrants met with a traveling Lutheran missionary in the home of Jorgen Eliason to organize the "Fordefjord Norwegian Evangelical Congregation of Poulsbo," named for the body of water at Eliason's childhood home. Eliason donated land for a church, which was built in 1887, and the adjacent hillside cemetery. In 1908 a larger, more substantial church was built by Martin Bjermeland, a skilled carpenter, at the cost of four thousand dollars. This building remains today, although in recent years major additions have been made.

Poulsbo is located at what was once called Dogfish Bay, now Liberty Bay. It was settled by Scandinavians; in 1882 it was reported that the town was 90 percent Norwegian. At first Poulsbo was involved principally with logging; later it became an important fishing community.

## Temple de Hirsch 1908

SEATTLE, KING COUNTY

In August 1889 about forty Ashkenazim (German and eastern European Jews) met at the courthouse in Seattle to organize a permanent congregation. A synagogue, Ohaveth Sholom, was built in 1892 at 8th Avenue and Seneca Street, but the congregation ceased to function in 1895 because of financial difficulties caused by the Panic of 1893. The building was then used as a public school until 1913.

In 1899 a Reform congregation, which included some of the members of that first Seattle congregation, was organized and designated Temple de Hirsch. Services were held in a small hall until 1901, when the members moved to their own temple although it was only partly completed. At that time they determined to build a larger temple at another site. The cornerstone was laid in March 1907 and in May the following year the large brick Temple de Hirsch, located in Seattle's Capitol Hill area, was dedicated. It was used by the Reform congregation until they moved into their new synagogue in 1960. At the present time the old sanctuary is used by a group of the Orthodox Bikur Cholim congregation.

A beautiful stained-glass window at the east end of the temple depicts Moses descending from Mount Sinai. He carries two tablets inscribed with the Decalogue (Ten Commandments).

## St. Joseph's Catholic Church 1909

KALAMA, COWLITZ COUNTY

When the Northern Pacific Railroad began its branch line from the Columbia to Puget Sound in 1870, it chose the present site of Kalama for its southern terminus. Immediately Kalama became a tent city and boom town, filled with speculators, railroad builders, and others ready to benefit from its quick growth. In 1872 the county seat was located at Kalama, where it remained for sixty years. The boom ended when the rail line was completed in 1873, but, in the years following, Kalama became a transportation center on the Columbia as the rail terminus for the railroad ferry and as a steamboat shipping point.

In 1874 an Oblate priest from Cowlitz Mission gathered a few Catholics together and built a small chapel. In 1889 it was the only church standing in Kalama after a disastrous fire swept through the town. In 1909 a Franciscan priest managed the construction of the present church, which was built on the site of the first small chapel. An early-day local newspaper reported that the church had a high-quality bell, main and side altars, choir loft, and organ. The church, which has since been remodeled and restored, stands on a steep hill overlooking the Columbia River and can easily be seen from Interstate 5.

## Bellingham Unitarian Fellowship   1910
### (originally Lutheran)

BELLINGHAM, WHATCOM COUNTY

In 1853 a few settlers took up donation land claims along the shores of Bellingham Bay after coal and a good source of waterpower were discovered nearby. Five years later, thousands of miners and others seeking an easy overland route to the recently discovered gold fields along the Fraser River in Canada flocked to the area. Sehome and Whatcom were quickly platted and for a few months were boom towns. When the adventurers found that the gold fields were inaccessible from Bellingham Bay, they left almost as quickly as they had come.

The surviving settlements, isolated from overland travel by foothills and dense forests, grew slowly until the late 1880s when railroad building and land speculation brought many people, including numerous foreign immigrants, to the region. In 1904 the four small towns that by then stood along the shore consolidated and became the city of Bellingham.

German-speaking Lutheran missionaries visited the area beginning in the 1880s, and by the turn of the century a congregation of German and German-Russian settlers was organized. Their church, named Evangelische Lutherische Kirche and designed by Seattle architect E. E. Ziegler, was built in 1910. The Reverend Friedrich Nitz, who came to Bellingham in 1907, acted as contractor. The twenty-nine-hundred-dollar cost of the building was mostly for materials since the greatest part of the labor was supplied by the pastor and the congregation. An important function in the early days of the church was the German language parochial school which met in the first floor of the building.

*First Church of Christ, Scientist*   1910

In 1884 a student of Mary Baker Eddy, organizer of the Church of Christ, Scientist, in Boston in 1879, visited Everett and addressed a small group. The following year another student of Mrs. Eddy came to live in Everett and opened her home for services and Sunday school. Later a rented hall served as a meeting place for several years. Two brothers from Oconto, Wisconsin, where their mother was a Christian Science practitioner, came to work in the logging industry and helped establish the church here. The First Church of Christ, Scientist, of Everett was incorporated in October 1899, with six charter members. A small building with a seating capacity of one hundred was erected by the members and used for services and as a reading room.

Three lots were purchased in 1907 and in 1910 the present church, which seats four hundred, was constructed. The dominant feature of this handsome frame building is its gleaming white façade. Like many other early Christian Science churches, but not a denominational requirement, it followed the Greek style: the stepped platform, the columns, and the pediment, ornamented here only by a small round window. The interior has an unusual and interesting seating arrangement: curved pews in a semicircular pattern face the reader's platform, which is in a recessed alcove on the long side of the large auditorium.

## St. Barbara's Catholic Church   1911

BLACK DIAMOND, KING COUNTY

Black Diamond was one of several coal-mining company towns near the Green River. Coal was hauled on the Columbia and Puget Sound Railroad through Renton to Seattle, where much of the coal was then shipped to San Francisco.

Benedictine fathers of St. Martin's Abbey (near Olympia) brought Catholic services to the many Italian and Austrian immigrants who had been recruited to work in the coal mines. A church site was donated and the building, which was financed by donations, was completed at a cost of $2,724. Father Aloysius Mlinar was the person most responsible for its construction. At the time of church dedication in 1913, flags from the Papal State, Austria, and the United States were flown. The unusual helm-shaped roof line at the base of the spire is repeated in the louvered openings of the bell tower. The bell was brought from the parish of Franklin, a former nearby town in the coal-field area.

## St. Joseph's Catholic Church 1911

Slovak

TACOMA, PIERCE COUNTY

Immigrants of many diverse national groups came to Tacoma, often clustering in neighborhood settlements, establishing lodges and churches. Many of these churches still stand, and some are used by the original ethnic group. St. Joseph's Slovak church is one of these. The first Slovakian family came to Tacoma in 1888: ten years later there were more than fifty. They organized several Slovakian societies and in 1906 petitioned Catholic Bishop Edward John O'Dea for a parish. When their request was granted, a central location was chosen so that Slovaks from every part of the city could attend. Lots were purchased for twenty-five hundred dollars. Construction of the church began in 1911 when the members themselves, laboring days and evenings after working at their regular jobs, excavated the basement and laid the foundation. After much effort and many sacrifices on the part of the people and their priest, the Reverend Aloysius Mlinar, the church was completed at a cost of twenty thousand dollars.

The pinnacles at the belfry corners, the crosses above the gables on the spire, and the feeling of solidity in this fine brick structure reflect the design of some of the churches of Czechoslovakia. The architect was C. Frank Mahon.

*First Christian Church*    1912

Disciples of Christ

CAMAS, CLARK COUNTY

The unusual octagonal design of this large frame church was patterned after the study of Alexander Campbell, one of the founders of the denomination. Fine stained glass is used in windows throughout the building, including the clerestory windows in the cupola.

The church was organized in 1911 by a group of about twenty people who had belonged to Christian churches elsewhere, most of them coming from Nebraska, Oklahoma, Iowa, Indiana, and Texas. A Bible school that met in the Odd Fellows Hall soon had a large attendance. A site was selected and plans were made to erect the largest church building in the town. Although the congregation planned first to build only the basement, the church board of extension granted a thousand-dollar loan so that the church could be completed. The total cost was forty-one hundred dollars, including the lot. At the dedication services fifteen hundred dollars was raised for the church, and evangelistic meetings held for five weeks increased the membership dramatically.

*First African*
*Methodist Episcopal Church*    1912

Among the first Americans to settle land north of the Columbia River was George Bush, a free black who came west in 1844. A few years later a group led by George Washington, a black who later founded the town of Centralia, took up land in Lewis County. In 1879 the post–Civil War census showed 207 blacks in Washington Territory; in 1890 there were 1,602, including farmers, businessmen, hotel keepers, lawyers, and real estate men. Most of them lived in the urban areas of Seattle, Tacoma, and Spokane and in the towns of Roslyn, Franklin, and Newcastle where many came to work in the coal mines.

In 1896, S. J. Collins, who was later a minister in Roslyn, organized a Sunday school which met at homes in Seattle. Four years later the First African Methodist Episcopal Church was organized by several dedicated men and a missionary preacher who had come to the Northwest in 1889. For a number of years worship services were held in a large house that was modified to serve as a church. On the site of this earlier church, the present large brick building was erected in 1912. The church has long been acclaimed for its choir.

*Our Lady of the Valley*
*& St. Ives Catholic Church*   1914

HARMONY, LEWIS COUNTY

This white church, framed by tall poplars, has green-painted trim that accents the Roman-arch design of window and belfry openings. It is situated on a wooded hillside near the gorge where the Cowlitz River enters Mayfield Lake on its southwesterly course toward the Columbia.

Beginning in 1910, priests from St. Francis Mission at Cowlitz Prairie occasionally visited pioneer settlers to say Mass and perform baptismal rites at private homes or at the Harmony schoolhouse. In 1914 ten Catholic families (Irish, German, and Polish) joined together to build a church at this site, which was central to their homes. Land was donated for a church and a cemetery. Enthusiastic parishioners worked hard to clear the land and help build the church under the supervision of a professional designer and builder. They received financial aid from the church extension society as well as many small donations, including some from banks in Chehalis and even from Sears, Roebuck Company in Seattle. Some of the lumber came from a nearby mill, but most supplies were hauled by wagon team from Chehalis, each trip taking two days. The women not only helped raise money but also helped finish and decorate the interior.

After completion of the church, young men made the two-day trip to Cowlitz Mission about once a month to bring a priest to offer Mass.

*Ocean Park*
*United Methodist Church*     1914

OCEAN PARK, PACIFIC COUNTY

Methodist ministers began holding regular services at Long Beach Peninsula settlements in 1871. An important part of the Methodist ministry throughout the United States was the traditional summer camp meeting. People from miles around gathered at a campsite to listen to preaching several times a day, to picnic, and to visit. In this tradition camp meetings were held on the peninsula. Prominent Methodists from the peninsula and Portland, Oregon, formed the Ocean Park Camp Meeting Association in 1883 to provide a Christian summer resort for the members. The association purchased 250 acres of land, including three-fourths of a mile of ocean frontage, and camp meetings were held there for a few years.

The church at Ocean Park, built by popular subscription with a Portland man matching all funds contributed, was started in 1913 and completed at a cost of $3,125 the following year, free of debt. It is an example of the "shingle style" design that became very popular for country estates and homes in the late 1800s. Within the large squat belfry is the bell from the Oysterville Methodist church that was destroyed by hurricane-force winds in 1921. The inscription on the bell reads: "First Methodist Episcopal Church, Oysterville, 1876."

## Our Lady of Mount Virgin Catholic Church  1915

This classically designed church is situated on a hillside in the Rainier Valley area of Seattle where many early Italian immigrants settled at the turn of the century. It is made of wood, although its design and many architectural details reflect the characteristics of stone and stucco buildings of northern Italy: the smooth, flush surfaces of the siding, the use of quoins at the corners, the different treatment of first and second stories, and the use of columns and other trim on the building's face.

Dedicated in 1915, it was built as a church and school after Father Louis Caramello came from Turin, Italy, in 1913 to work among Italian immigrants in the community. The church was named for the parish in Italy that was the origin of many of the immigrants. The beautiful stained-glass windows in the sanctuary memorialize many of the early members.

Although still an Italian parish, the church now also serves several other ethnic groups in the neighborhood.

## Fir-Conway Lutheran Church     1916

CONWAY, SKAGIT COUNTY

Beginning in 1880 a Norwegian Lutheran minister, the Reverend Christian Jorgenson of Stanwood, visited settlers in the rich delta land of the South Fork of the Skagit River, holding services in homes and schoolhouses. In 1888 a congregation called Den Evangeliske Lutherske Menighed of Skagit was organized. At that time most worshipers walked to the services, with a few coming by rowboat or by wagon. Later the congregation purchased a half acre of diked farm land across the river from the present town of Conway, and in 1896 the outside shell of a 24-by-42-foot church building was constructed. It was put into use immediately even though it was not fully completed until 1902, when it was dedicated. In 1916 a new, larger church, the present structure, was erected, with a seating capacity of 350. The church was built high off the ground because of flood danger from the nearby Skagit. When the church was dedicated many people arrived by automobile, traveling on improved roads and across the new bridge.

Across the river, the Conway Norwegian Evangelical Congregation was organized in 1895 in the town that had been platted a few years earlier when the Great Northern Railroad was built through the valley. For ten years a pastor from Bellingham came each Sunday to minister to the congregation. Their church was built in 1905. In 1917, a few years after the bridge was completed, the two Lutheran congregations joined together to become the Fir-Conway Lutheran Church.

## Holy Cross Polish National Catholic Church 1916

PE ELL, LEWIS COUNTY

In the early 1850s Bohemian settlers took up donation land claims in an isolated area of western Lewis County near the banks of the upper Chehalis River. The claims were a few miles from an area known then as Pe Ell Prairie. A French-Canadian, Pierre Charles, had kept his horses there and the Indians had named the prairie for him. Pierre, with the Indian pronunciation, became Pe Ell. Forty years later, Omar Mauerman, son of one of these pioneer settlers, platted the town of Pe Ell at the time of construction of the Northern Pacific branch line connecting Chehalis Junction with South Bend on the Willapa River. The branch line made possible the development of a vast new timbered area. Among the people who came to work in logging camps and sawmills and to take up claims in the newly opened area were large numbers of German and Polish immigrants, many of whom had first lived in Minnesota, Michigan, and Wisconsin. Pe Ell became known as a strong Polish Catholic community. In 1892 Catholics there asked for a Polish priest; their first church was dedicated the next year. By 1902 a larger Roman Catholic church was built, served by a Polish priest.

However, near the turn of the century in the United States, some Poles broke from the Roman Catholic church and formed the Polish National Catholic Church to maintain their own language and traditions. Holy Cross, built in 1916 and still in use, is one of the few of this denomination west of the Mississippi.

# EASTERN WASHINGTON CHURCHES

## St. Paul's Mission  1847
Catholic

KETTLE FALLS, STEVENS COUNTY

The first white men to visit Kettle Falls on the Columbia River, a favorite salmon fishing ground for generations of many Indian tribes, were a group of explorers and fur traders from Montreal in 1811. In 1825 the Hudson's Bay Company built Fort Colville, a trading post that became the center of the fur trade east of the Cascades and was visited by explorers, scientists, and missionaries.

Historic St. Paul's Mission, near old Fort Colville, was founded in 1845 by Father Pierre Jean DeSmet, the famous Jesuit priest from Belgium who worked among the Indian tribes of the Rocky Mountain area for many years. The small chapel built at that time was replaced in 1847 by a larger building that was constructed under the direction of Father Joseph Joset. For over twenty years during fur trade times it was a cultural center for the Indians and white population there. It was abandoned when the Hudson's Bay Company moved its operations to Canada in 1870.

The building pictured is a later restoration which used much of the original material. The structure is fur-trade-style "post in the sill," in which timbers were laid horizontally in the spaces between posts. The timbers were tongued at the ends to fit into vertical slots in the posts and secured with wooden pins. In the 1930s the building was relocated to a nearby site when land near Kettle Falls was vacated for Roosevelt Lake, which holds the backwater of Coulee Dam. The mission site was made a Washington State Park in 1951.

## St. Joseph's Mission    1869

Catholic

TAMPICO, YAKIMA COUNTY

The church at St. Joseph's Mission was built in 1869 by Father L. N. St. Onge and J. B. Boulet, a teacher and later a priest, both of whom had come from Quebec to Washington Territory to work among the Indians. Father St. Onge came to the site on Ahtanum Creek in 1867 to re-establish a mission begun twenty years earlier by French Oblate missionaries. This first mission was maintained until 1855 when it was burned by United States soldiers during the Indian wars in the territory.

When Father St. Onge came he built a log house, 16 by 24 feet, which he used for a church and a home. In 1868, after Boulet joined him, they planted an orchard and garden and started a school for Indian children. The next year they decided they needed a larger church. St. Onge and others went twelve miles upstream to cut logs that were then hand hewn into heavy timbers and laid up to form solid walls. The timbers were locked together at the corners of the building with dovetail joints. The two missionaries worked at the construction until the priest, who had injured himself, had to return to the East Coast, leaving Boulet to complete the task. Jesuit priests took over the mission, which later was abandoned and fell into disrepair. It was reconstructed and dedicated in 1919, and the buildings, standing in the old orchard, are much the same as when they were first used.

134

## Dixie Christian Church    1883

Disciples of Christ

DIXIE, WALLA WALLA COUNTY

Dixie is a small farming community about ten miles northeast of Walla Walla. In the late 1850s, after the treaties had been signed with eastern Washington Indian tribes, white settlers, mostly from the Midwest, began to take up land in this predominantly dry country. In the early sixties the three Kershaw brothers, known for their singing of the song "Dixie" as they crossed the prairies toward Oregon, settled on land at the confluence of Mud and Dry creeks. Their homestead land soon became known as Dixie Crossing, later shortened to Dixie.

Several miles from the present town of Dixie, a group of pioneer Disciples of Christ from the Midwest organized a congregation in about 1857. They moved to Dixie in 1876, first meeting in a schoolhouse before the present small frame church was built. It is the oldest standing Christian church in Washington. The design is severely simple and without ornamentation. The church was first served by a pastor from Waitsburg, beginning in 1884.

## Ahtanum Pioneer Church    1884
(originally Congregational)

AHTANUM, YAKIMA COUNTY

The E. S. Tanner family, originally from Connecticut, came from Oregon to the Ahtanum Valley in 1870. They sought out other families and organized a Sunday school that met in the Tanner home. In 1873 nine people organized a Congregational church, the fourth in the territory. Ministers from Walla Walla or The Dalles, Oregon, came once a month to preach at services held in a log schoolhouse.

In 1883 plans were made to build a church; almost $1,000 was pledged, and land and labor were donated. The church, which cost $1,894, was dedicated the next year. Contributions from friends and relatives in New York and Illinois and a Sunday school in Connecticut paid for the pulpit, chairs, and a chandelier. The bell, which was also a gift of eastern friends, was cast in Troy, New York, and placed in the belfry in 1886. The shingled steeple is topped by an intricate finial of wood and a handsome wrought iron weather vane made by a blacksmith in Union Gap.

A new church has recently been built on adjacent property by the present congregation, an independent denomination.

## Asotin United Methodist Church    ca. 1889

ASOTIN, ASOTIN COUNTY

Settlers began coming to the flat land on the Snake River near present-day Asotin in the late 1870s, after the end of the Nez Perce war. In 1883 the territorial legislature created Asotin County. There were two small towns on the Snake River only a mile apart and citizens of each wanted to have the county seat. However, after property midway between them was offered for county use, the people put aside their differences and the towns merged. Asotin became county seat and remains so today. T. M. E. Schank and William H. Reed, who donated the land for the courthouse, also gave a nearby site for a Methodist church and parsonage in 1884. Even though there were poor crops and the people had little money during the next few years, the small congregation built a parsonage. A short time later they were able to build this frame church when the church extension society helped them with a $250 building grant.

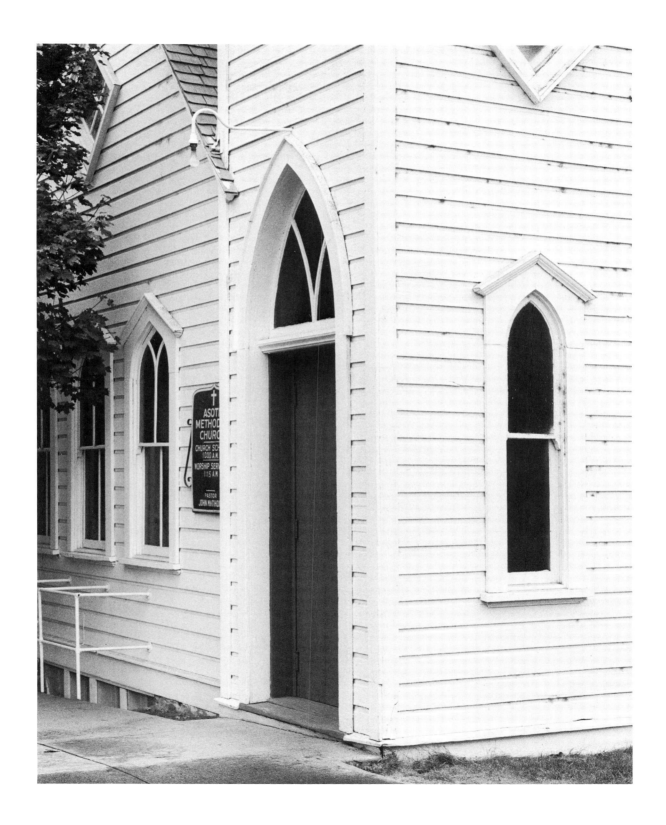

*First Baptist Church—Conservative*    1890

DAYTON, COLUMBIA COUNTY

A Baptist congregation was organized in Dayton in 1872 and the first church, a frame structure, was built in 1878. Twelve years later the growing congregation built the present church. The basic structure is red brick which was manufactured in the area. The open belfry is, surprisingly, wood but its fine decorative elements complement the brick ornamentation below the belfry and roof edges.

After the Civil War, settlers, many from Missouri, took up land along the Touchet River, and in 1871 the town of Dayton was platted near an old Indian campsite. The favorable location on stage routes brought quick growth and prosperity. The local economy included flour, woolen, and planing mills, and, it is said, nineteen saloons in spite of the fact that many citizens wanted a temperance town. In 1875, when Columbia County was created from part of Walla Walla County, Dayton was named county seat.

## Holy Trinity Episcopal Church  1895

PALOUSE, WHITMAN COUNTY

This small, attractive church, designed after an English church, has white siding and brown-shingled buttresses. The beautiful window detail, including stained glass, is accented by dark green window frames. An unusual feature of the church yard entrance and seldom seen in the United States is the lich gate. Traditionally the bier is placed under its roof to await the arrival of the clergyman to conduct the funeral service.

Beginning in 1879 Episcopal church services were held in a public hall whenever a minister or bishop passed through Palouse on his circuit. In 1891 a mission church was established with services held twice a month. At that time Palouse was a rough sawmill town with a dozen saloons. The churches in the town were supported by only a few men and women. In spite of the fact that the country was suffering from the Panic of 1893, Episcopalians began construction of their church on donated property on the hillside above the town. Building funds were lost when local banks failed in 1895. Members persevered, however, and the church was completed and was consecrated on December 25, 1895, in services conducted by the pioneer eastern Washington missionary, Bishop Lemuel H. Wells.

## Cedonia Union Church     1897

CEDONIA, STEVENS COUNTY

A group of people of varied backgrounds, mostly farmers from the Midwest, people of German, Scottish, and French descent, joined together to build this small community church. Money for the building was raised by subscription and, in addition, founders and friends of the church donated 114 days of labor, resulting in the building being completed debt free. The church was dedicated by a German Lutheran minister, but ten years later the congregation was organized as a Christian church since most of the community at that time were of that faith.

At about the same time the church was being built, three of the church founders, G. E. Cornwall, Robert Dashiell, and Martin Scatten, were chosen as a committee to select a new name for the community, which had been known as Harney Creek. At first they picked the name Macedonia, from the Bible verse "Come over to Macedonia and help us," because they were struggling to build their new church. Macedonia, however, seemed too long a name so they shortened it to Cedonia.

The church is fairly narrow and the wide tower of the belfry placed at one side of the building gives the front an unusual, unbalanced appearance. The bell was donated by a merchant in nearby Hunters; the pews and pulpit were made by the original builders, who probably were also the designers of the church.

## St. Andrew's Episcopal Church    1898

CHELAN, CHELAN COUNTY

St. Andrew's was organized as the result of visits to Chelan by Bishop Lemuel H. Wells beginning in 1889. In 1894 he brought the Reverend Brian Roberts, a missionary serving other places in the area, to serve at Chelan. According to church records, Roberts, with the help of his father, a wealthy Bostonian, obtained plans for this handsome log church from Stanford White, noted East Coast architect, who designed the church without ever coming to the Northwest.

Local Episcopalians established a logging camp to provide logs for the church as well as money for its construction. The building site and much of the labor were donated. Teams of horses were used to haul the logs from the logging camp down to the lake, where they were towed by the steamboat *Stehekin* to the town.

In 1897 the stone foundation was laid and construction began on the church. The first service was held on Christmas Eve, 1898. It was a "stand-up" service since the seats were not yet installed. The seats, as well as the bell tower, were added the next year. The exterior and interior have been well maintained in essentially original condition.

## Ritzville Zion
## United Church of Christ    1901

RITZVILLE, ADAMS COUNTY

The shingled cylindrical turrets at each corner of the belfry and at the front corners of the main roof are the most distinctive feature of this church. Also unusual are the spherical metal finials on top of the turrets and steeple.

Immigrants, some of whom came directly from Germany and others who first settled in Illinois, organized the German Evangelical Zion Church in 1888. Later the small mission church joined the German Congregational conference. The present building was completed in 1901 at a cost of six thousand dollars. The German language was used for almost fifty years until a complete transition was made to English.

The first settlers came to the area in 1878. In the 1880s railroads and development companies conducted an intensive promotional program in Europe and in the Midwest to bring German and German-Russian farmers to homestead the agricultural lands that were being made accessible. Ritzville, a milling and wheat-shipping center on the main line of the Northern Pacific Railroad, grew rapidly.

The foreign born in Adams County as shown in the 1910 census included 130 Swedes, 475 Germans, and 1,264 Russians.

## Mary Queen of Heaven
## Catholic Church    1902

SPRAGUE, LINCOLN COUNTY

The gleaming white spire of this imposing solid brick church, built on a hillside overlooking the town, can be seen from a distance of several miles. The church was designed by architect Herman Preusse, who charged a fee of $350 but then gave $100 to the building fund. The building, 87 by 36 feet with seating for three hundred people, cost $10,000 and replaced a smaller wood church built in 1883. The buttressed walls, apse, and stained-glass windows, which were gifts from several members, reflect European cathedral architecture.

Sprague developed rapidly beginning in 1880 when the Northern Pacific Railroad chose that location for a division point and construction center. Many German, Italian, and Irish railroad workers settled in the area, and in a short time there were 250 Catholic families in the large, seventy-mile-square parish. In 1887 St. Joseph's Academy, a Catholic boarding school, opened and soon had 100 pupils. The town, including the railroad shops, was almost totally destroyed by fire in 1895. When the Northern Pacific moved its operations to Spokane, most of the town's population left. However, good crops and high prices brought prosperity to the farming area and Sprague regained some of its importance.

*Touchet Community*
*Congregational Church*     1902
TOUCHET, WALLA WALLA COUNTY

Touchet is a small town located at the confluence of the Walla Walla and Touchet rivers, between the Columbia River site of Hudson's Bay Company's old Fort Walla Walla and the Whitman Mission near present-day Walla Walla. During the Idaho gold rush, stage coach lines followed this route, and a stage station and a hotel were established here in the early 1860s. Dr. Dorsey Baker chose the same route for his narrow-gauge, strap-iron railroad which, when completed in 1875, connected Walla Walla with Columbia River steamboats. John Hill's house was used as a stop until 1882 when a depot was built. In 1884 Hill platted a town of a few blocks which included two stores, a post office, and a one-room school. The town began to flourish a few years later after irrigation made the surrounding area highly productive.

Congregationalists who organized in Touchet in 1897, and for five years met in the schoolhouse, built this small frame church in 1902. The open belfry, which allows a good view of the fine old bell, is topped by an unusual ornamental metal finial which was donated by one of the residents of the town.

A Village Missions pastor now leads the congregation.

*Assembly of God*
*Community Church*    ca. 1905
(originally Presbyterian)

CONNELL, FRANKLIN COUNTY

Cut boards that form a distinctive arch, fancy shingles, and large windows divided into Gothic and diamond shapes ornament the gables of this hip-roof frame church. The large corner entrance tower set at an angle to the face of the building, the octagonal belfry with tall arched openings, the spire with fancy-cut shingles, and the small cupola atop the roof are other interesting design features. W. A. Campbell, a pioneer merchant, and his wife, Iola, were largely responsible for the organization of the church at a time of growth and expansion by Presbyterians in eastern Washington.

The church stands on a hillside overlooking the farming and grain-shipping community of Connell. The town, in a wheat-producing belt, grew at the junction of the Oregon Railroad and Navigation Company and the Northern Pacific Railroad lines.

*Zion United Methodist Church of Rocklyn* 1905

ROCKLYN, LINCOLN COUNTY

This fine frame church with its tall steeple stands alone on a rise in the rolling wheat farm land near the grain-shipping station of Rocklyn, west of Davenport. Here, in the early 1880s, not far from the main line of the Northern Pacific, a number of German-speaking families took up homestead land to raise crops and cattle. They had come from Minnesota, which they felt was then becoming too crowded. In 1883 six men organized a Methodist congregation, and the first services were held in the home of Mr. and Mrs. Gottlieb Mielke. Mielke and his son Edward donated land for a church, which was built in 1889; it was replaced by the present building in 1905. All religious services were conducted in German until the late 1920s.

## St. Boniface Catholic Church 1905

UNIONTOWN, WHITMAN COUNTY

This impressive, large, red-brick church with twin spires stands on the north hillside overlooking Uniontown, a small town in the southeastern corner of Whitman County. The church was built by German Catholic immigrants who came from Minnesota to settle farm lands in Washington Territory.

Jesuit priests came from their mission in Lapwaii, Idaho, to conduct religious services for the newcomers, and in 1879 Father Joseph Cataldo organized St. Boniface church. He also suggested the name Uniontown for the settlement because it was near Union Flat Creek and also a junction for travel routes through the area.

In 1893 the foundation was laid for a large church in the then prosperous community. However, a series of crop failures and financial depression halted construction for over ten years. The present church, smaller than originally planned, was started in 1904 and completed the following year at a cost of about twenty thousand dollars. The structure is 57 by 140 feet and is built in the shape of a cross in Roman style. Beautiful stained-glass windows are used throughout. The interior surfaces of plaster are richly ornamented with painted decoration and carvings. The architect was Herman Preusse of Spokane.

*First Christian Church*     1905

Disciples of Christ

WAITSBURG, WALLA WALLA COUNTY

A settlement at the delta of Copper Creek and the Touchet River on an overland travel route became the site for Waitsburg. In 1864 Sylvester Wait, for whom the town was later named, built the first flour mill to process wheat grown in the nearby farm land.

Disciples of Christ in the vicinity were meeting as early as 1867. By 1876 two churches had been organized in country districts near Waitsburg and preaching services were held in the town's schoolhouse when visiting evangelists passed through. In 1883 a church consolidating the three congregations was organized in Waitsburg. For a year the sixty members and a large Sunday school met in the Methodist church until their own building was completed.

The present church, built at a cost of about fifteen thousand dollars, was dedicated in February 1906. A special train brought 150 guests from Walla Walla to help celebrate the occasion. The large frame church includes a considerable variety in design and ornamentation, including an open belfry, corner tower, fancy-cut shingles, classic wreath and garland details over the windows, and elaborate metal finials.

## St. Mary of the Rosary Catholic Church    1906

CHEWELAH, STEVENS COUNTY

In 1859, during gold rush times, a public inn was opened in the Colville River valley near present-day Chewelah on the old overland trail used for years by Indians, explorers, traders, missionaries, miners, soldiers, and other travelers. A few white settlers who raised stock and hay, cut timber, or searched for gold homesteaded nearby. Then, in the early 1880s, the discovery of large deposits of lead and silver brought large mining companies and an increased population to the area. Stagecoach, freight wagon, mule train, or horseback continued to be the means of transport until 1889, when the Spokane Falls and Northern Railroad was built.

Father Aloysius Folchi, a Jesuit priest who traveled north from Spokane in his missionary work, founded the first Catholic church in Chewelah in 1885. He purchased an old log building, a former trading post on the historic wagon trail, for use as a church. The next year a small frame church, 20 by 35 feet, was built on donated land. Twenty years later James Monahan donated a new building site and the present church was built under the guidance of Father Aloysius van der Velden. It served a congregation of Indians, and Irish, German, Slovenian, and Luxemburgian settlers. Various improvements and changes have been made in later years, mostly to the entrance and interior. A distinctive feature of the church is the slender, octagonal steeple, ornamented on each face with a gable above a louvered panel.

*Christ Lutheran Church*    1906

EGYPT, LINCOLN COUNTY

This well-cared-for, traditional German Lutheran church stands in the hilly, thinly settled area of the wheat belt north of Davenport. In 1881 a few German farmers came here from Minnesota, traveling on foot or by wagon train, seeking land for homesteads. In 1890 a pastor from Spokane conducted worship services in the home of Andrew Reinbold, one of that first group who came in 1881. The eight men who attended the services organized a church that day. A pastor from Davenport served the congregation, which for many years met in the schoolhouse.

The church was built in 1906; materials were purchased in Spokane and hauled to the construction site by members. The church was used only for religious services and the congregation followed German tradition: men sat on one side of the church, women and children on the other. Reflecting another German tradition, in 1911 the pastor organized a brass band from among the congregation. Services were conducted in German. English services were added in 1911 and fourteen years later all services were conducted in English. In 1957 the church was turned to face the nearby highway and various improvements were also made at that time.

*Rosalia Christian Church*     1910

Disciples of Christ

ROSALIA, WHITMAN COUNTY

Disciples of Christ built this substantial brick church in 1910 with the help of a fifteen-hundred-dollar loan from the church extension board. The heavy four-sided tower is topped by an interesting and unusual smaller, octagonal, and almost onion-shaped cupola.

Fourteen people led by evangelist W. E. Richardson, a school teacher and later a lawyer in Spokane, organized the congregation in 1887. Church services were first held in a schoolhouse and then in a hall after the congregation shared for a brief time a frame building constructed by the community and dedicated by the United Brethren. This building was purchased in 1899 and used until the present church was erected. During these years the congregation had no resident pastor but was served by "circuit rider" visiting ministers.

Settlement began at the site of Rosalia in the late 1860s, and the town was named in 1872. By 1907 three rail lines passed through Rosalia, trade center and railroad transfer point in this prosperous farm area.

## St. James Episcopal Church    1912

BREWSTER, OKANOGAN COUNTY

Brewster is near old Fort Okanogan. The fort, established in 1811 by the Astor Fur Company, was under the control of Canadians from 1813 until it was abandoned after the boundary treaty of 1846. From the earliest times many Canadians and British settled in this area.

The heritage of these settlers can be seen in the English-style architecture of this fine stone church—the heavy crenalated tower, casement windows, and overhanging roof of the exterior and the stone walls, lack of adornment, and exposed beam structure of the interior.

The church was started in 1911 after Mrs. Josephine McKinley of Brewster received a commitment from Great Northern Railroad officials that extra stone, blasted from hillsides to create a roadbed, would be donated for a church. The stone was carried by stone-boat from as far away as Chelan and then hauled to the building site by horse-drawn sleds. Volunteer masons laid up the stone.

*St. James Catholic Church*     1915

HUNTERS, STEVENS COUNTY

One of the most unusual of belfries is this one—shaped in the form of a bell. A Catholic bishop, who traveled through the area while visiting the Colville Indian Reservation in 1914, arranged to have the church built in Hunters. For many years it was cared for by Jesuit priests, but it is no longer used. It stands beside the highway that is the transportation route between Davenport and British Columbia. Hunters, located on a creek of the same name, was one of several early settlements on the east bank of the Columbia, across from the Colville Reservation. Miners and adventurers traveled on the river, moving inland along creeks and streams in their search for gold and silver in the hill country of Stevens County during the late 1800s.

*Pioneer Church*     1916

Independent

(originally German-Russian Congregational)

ODESSA, LINCOLN COUNTY

This church, which has such a striking belfry, was built by descendants of Germans who had migrated to provinces along the Volga River in eastern Russia in the late 1700s. One hundred years later these descendants left Russia to come to the United States, most of them settling in the farm lands of Nebraska. When railroads opened new lands in the West for settlement, many of these German-Russians came to the Big Bend country of eastern Washington. In 1892 the Great Northern Railroad was built through the area. Odessa, the name of a well-known city in the wheat belt of Russia, was chosen as a suitable name for one of the towns platted along the railroad's line in the great wheat-farming district recently settled by the immigrants.

The church, originally named St. Matthew's, was built by Conrad Eckhardt, who followed traditions of churches of the congregation in Germany and Russia. The open frame of the distinctive belfry is topped by a smooth-surfaced, high metal dome and unusual pinnacles at the corners of the roof.

# Bibliography

PUBLISHED SOURCES

"Adams County." *Ritzville Journal Times,* Washington Pioneer Edition, 1949.

Adatto, Albert. "Sephardim and the Seattle Sephardic Community." Master's thesis, University of Washington, 1939.

*American Jewish Yearbook.* Philadelphia: Jewish Publications Society of America, 1899–.

Andrews, Theodore. *The Polish National Catholic Church of America and Poland.* London: SPCK, 1953.

Atwood, Rev. Albert. *Glimpses of Pioneer Life on Puget Sound.* Seattle: Denton Coryell Co., 1903.

Baeder, Louis. *Outline of the Development of Early American Architecture.* N.p.: State of Washington, 1937.

Baker, Rev. J. C. *Baptist History of the North Pacific Coast.* Philadelphia: American Baptist Publication Society, 1912.

Baker, W. W. *Forty Years a Pioneer.* Seattle: Lowman and Hanford, 1934.

Bancroft, H. H. *History of Washington, Idaho and Montana, 1845–89.* San Francisco: The History Co., 1890.

Barnett, Homer Garner. *Indian Shakers: A Messianic Cult of the Pacific Northwest.* Carbondale: Southern Illinois University Press, 1957.

Bischoff, William N., S. J. *The Jesuits in Old Oregon 1840–1940.* Caldwell, Id.: Caxton Printers, 1945.

Blaine, Catherine, and Rev. David E. Blaine. "Letters from the Pacific Northwest, written by David E. Blaine and Kate P. Blaine, 1853–1858." Reproduced from typewritten copy. Northwest Collection, Suzzallo Library.

Blanchet, Francis Norbert. *Historical Sketches of the Catholic Church in Oregon, during the Past Forty Years.* Portland: Catholic Sentinel Press, 1878.

Bowden, Angie Burt. *Early Schools of Washington Territory.* Seattle: Lowman and Hanford Co., 1935.

Boulet, J. P. "The Story of the Missionary." *Fairhaven Herald* (Bellingham), January 25, 1904.

Boyd, Robert. *History of the Synod of Washington of the Presbyterian Church in the United States of America, 1835–1909.* Published by the Synod, 1910.

Brenna, Paulo. *Interessi Dell' Emigrazione Italiana Negli Stati Di Washington, Oregon, Idaho, e Montana. . . .* Rome: Tipografia Cartiere Centrali, 1916.

Brosnan, Cornelius J. *Jason Lee: Prophet of the New Oregon.* New York: Macmillan Co., 1932.

Buchanan, Charles Milton. "E. C. Chirouse." *The Indian Sentinel,* vol. 1, no. 7. Washington, D.C.: Bureau of Catholic Missions, 1918.

Burke, Arthur E., et al. *Architectural and Building Trades Dictionary.* Chicago: American Technical Society, 1950.

*The Coast* (also *Wilhelm's Magazine*). Seattle: Coast Publishing Co., 1901–11.

Conner, Louisa A. "Louisa Conner Story." *Puget Sound Mail* (LaConner), August 7, 1952.

Cronin, Kay. *Cross in the Wilderness.* Vancouver, B.C.: Mitchell Press, 1960.

Gaffney, Joseph W., in collaboration with Celia Jans. *A History of Sprague, 1880–1962.* Spokane[?], 1962.

Garth, Thos. R., Jr. "Early Architecture in the Northwest." *Pacific Northwest Quarterly,* 38, no. 3 (1947): 215–32.

Gaustad, Edwin Scott. *A Religious History of America.* New York: Harper and Row, 1966.

Goodykoontz, Colin B. *Home Missions on the American Frontier.* Caldwell, Id.: Caxton Printers, 1939.

Howell, Erle. *Methodism in the Northwest.* Nashville, Tenn.: Parthenon Press, 1966.

Jessett, Thomas E. *Pioneering God's Country: The History of the Diocese of Olympia, 1853–1953.* Tacoma: Church Lantern Press, 1953.

Kennedy, George W. *The Pioneer Campfire.* Portland: Clarke-Kundret Printing Co., 1914.

Lewis, William, ed. "Letters and Diaries of Rev. Elkanah and Mary Walker, 1839–52." Spokane, Wash.: Spokane Historical Society, 1917. Typed manuscript.

Mary Louise, Sister (Nellie Sullivan). "Eugene Casimir Chirouse, O.M.I., and the Indians of Washington." Master's thesis, University of Washington, 1932.

Mattila, Walter, ed. "The Lewis River Finns." *Cowlitz County Historical Quarterly,* 15, no. 1 (1973): 11–15.

McDonald, Lucile Saunders. *Coast Country: A History of Southwest Washington.* Portland: Binfords and Mort, 1966.

McNemee, A. J. *"Brother Mack," the Frontier Preacher: A Brief Record of the Difficulties and Hardships of a Pioneer Itinerant.* Portland: T. G. Robison, 1924.

Meany, Edmond S. *Origin of Washington Geographic Names.* Seattle: University of Washington Press, 1923.

Meeker, Ezra. *Washington Territory West of the Cascade Mountains.* Olympia, W.T.: Printed in the Transcript Office, 1870.

————. *Seventy Years of Progress in Washington.* Tacoma: Allstrom Printing Co., 1921.

Melton, Wm. Ray. *The Lumber Industry of Washington.* Tacoma: National Youth Administration of Washington, 1938.

Metz, W. J. "History of the Catholic Church and Schools in Washington." Assembled by Herman John Winter. N.p., 1936.

Miller, Wallace J. *Southwestern Washington.* Olympia: Pacific Publishing Co., 1890.

"Negroes in Washington." *The Republican* (Seattle), vol. 2, no. 34, Jan. 4, 1896.

Oliphant, James Orin. "Some Neglected Aspects of the History of the Pacific Northwest." *Pacific Northwest Quarterly,* 61, no. 1 (1970): 1–9.

————, and Ambrose Saricks, Jr. "Baptist and Other Missionary Labors in the Northwest, 1865–1890." *Pacific Northwest Quarterly,* 41, no. 4 (1950): 121–61.

Olsen, Mrs. Nels, ed. *The Willapa Country History Report.* Raymond, Wash.: Raymond Herald & Advertiser, 1965.

"Opportunities." (Brochure of the Northern Pacific Railroad.) St. Paul, 1910.

"The Pacific Northwest: A Guide for Settlers and Travelers." (Brochure of the Northern Pacific Railroad.) New York, 1882.

Peterson, Orval D. *Washington–Northern Idaho Disciples.* St. Louis, Mo.: Christian Board of Publication, 1945.

Polk, R. L., and Co. *Oregon, Washington and Idaho Gazetteer and Business Directory.* Vol. 1, 1884–85. Chicago, Ill.: R. L. Polk and Co. and A. C. Danser.

————. *Oregon, Washington and Idaho Gazetteer and Business Directory.* Vol. 4, 1889–90. Portland, Ore.: R. L. Polk and Co.

Prosch, Charles. *Reminiscences of Washington Territory.* Seattle, Wash.: 1904.

Reuss, Carl F. "Pioneers of Lincoln County: A Study in Migration." *Pacific Northwest Quarterly,* 30, no. 1 (1939): 51–64.

Sampson, Martin J. *Indians of Skagit County.* Mount Vernon, Wash.: Skagit County Historical Society, 1972.

Scammon, Charles M. "Lumbering in Washington Territory." *Overland Monthly* (San Francisco), vol. 5, no. 1, July 1870.

Schoenberg, Wilfred P. *A Chronicle of the Catholic History of the Pacific Northwest, 1743–1960.* Spokane: Gonzaga Preparatory School, 1962.

Smith, Dwight C. *Where the Saints Have Trod: Congregationalism in Washington since 1838.* Seattle: Frayn Printing Co., 1938.

*South Bend Journal.* South Bend, Wash. 1900.

Stine, Thomas Ostenson. *Scandinavians on the Pacific, Puget Sound.* Seattle: 1900.

*United States Census. Supplement for Washington.* 1910.

United States Census Publications. *Reports of Religious Bodies.* 1906, 1916.

Vaughn, Thomas, ed. *Space, Style, and Structure: Building in Northwest America.* Portland: Oregon Historical Society, 1974.

Waddell, Oscar M. *Eastern Washington Historical Primer.* Spokane: Eastern Washington State Historical Society, 1943.

"Washington." *Universal Jewish Encyclopedia,* 10: 468–69. New York, 1943.

Williams, L. R. *Our Pacific County.* Raymond, Wash.: The Raymond Herald, 1930.

Winser, H. J. *The Great Northwest: A Guide Book and Itinerary for the Use of Travelers of the Northern Pacific Railroad.* St. Paul: Riley Brothers, 1886.

Works Progress Administration, State of Wash. *Washington: A Guide to the Evergreen State.* Portland: Binfords and Mort, 1941.

———. *Told by the Pioneers.* 3 vols. 1937–38.

MISCELLANEOUS SOURCES

*Tacoma:*

University of Puget Sound. Methodist Archives.

Tacoma Public Library. Immigrant Interviews.

*Seattle:*

University of Washington, Suzzallo Library:
    Northwest Collection:
        Meany Pioneer File
        Pacific Northwest Regional Newspaper and Periodical Index
        Pamphlet Files: County, City, Biography, etc.
        Scrapbooks: Bagley, Dubuar, Eldridge Morse
    Manuscripts Division:
        Congregational Church Collection
        Jewish Collection
        Scandinavian Collection

United States Federal Archives. Census Report. 1900.

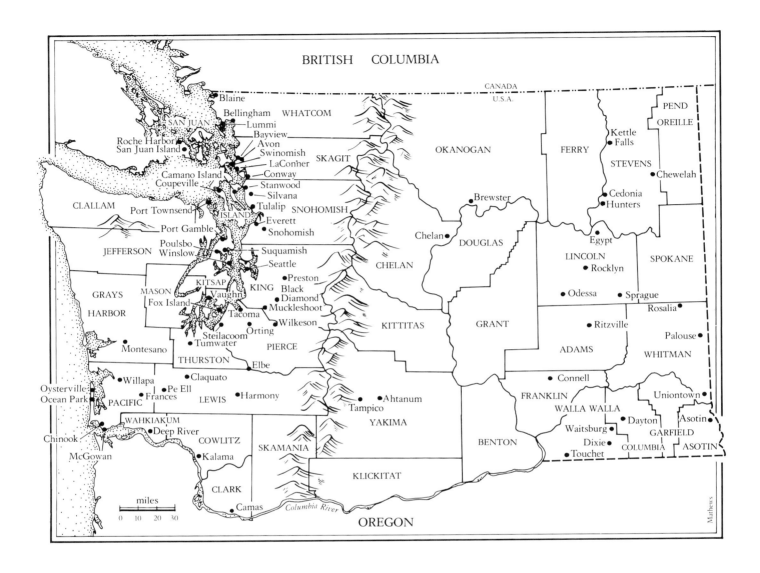

*Locations of churches pictured*

# Index

Churches are listed by town, with the county in parentheses.

* On State Register of Historic Places.
† On State and National Registers of Historic Places.